THE WATERS OF YELLOWSTONE

With Rod and Fly

THE WATERS OF YELLOWSTONE

With Rod and Fly

By

HOWARD BACK

Introduction by Craig Mathews

Afterword by Robert H. Berls

Photographs by Dan Callaghan

THE LYONS PRESS

Originally published in 1938 by Dodd, Mead, and Company, Inc.

First Lyons Press Edition 2000

Printed in the United States of America

Library of Congress Cataloging-in-Publication Data

CONTENTS

FOREWORD

It has been more than sixty years since Howard Back first published his delightful *The Waters of Yellowstone with Rod and Fly*, and twenty years have passed since a friend presented me a copy as a birthday gift. My treasured first edition with faded dust jacket, brittle pages, and failed bindings still occupies the "first place" position on my fly-tying desk. The desk sits in the den of my home six miles west of Yellowstone National Park, near West Yellowstone, Montana. From here I can see Hebgen Lake, and the South Fork of the Madison River is within two miles of our front door. Both of these famous waters are featured in Back's little guidebook, two of the many fine waters of Yellowstone country he brings the reader. The margins of my copy are filled with my notes, and the previous owner had underlined many of its key passages. Each winter I re-read this book and discover more of the author's fly-fishing secrets and share the pleasures he found in the waters of Yellowstone in 1938.

Howard Back was one of the first fly-fishing authors to bring the magical waters of Yellowstone Country to the attention of other anglers and the world. He described the Firehole River with her slow, rich currents, and prolific insect life, with its trout rising to mayflies and caddis near trailing weeds and undercut banks. He reported the sulfur fumes and steam rising high above its meadows while geysers erupt and fly fishers cast a worried and observant eye toward these thermal features.

He talked of the lovely South Fork of the Madison River—incredibly clear and cold; the Madison River, a huge chalk stream, from its birthplace at the junction of the Firehole and Gibbon Rivers downstream to Hebgen Lake and beyond; the Gibbon, its meandering meadow stretches separated by rough and tumble canyon sections, each filled with a mixed bag of trout and rare Montana grayling. Howard Back brought fly fishers his honest assessments of important Yellowstone rivers and streams like the Lamar, Gallatin, Soda Butte, Duck, Slough, Yellowstone, and Bechler River. He enticed readers to fish the lakes and ponds of the area and make you want to know and fish them.

Up until now, too few fishermen experiencing this "last best trout fishing place" have been able to share Howard Back's important work. The rare, first edition printed in 1938 was a limited printing and the only production of the book available. Anyone who has a love of Yellowstone fly fishing owes a debt to Nick Lyons of the Lyons Press for re-publishing Howard Back's book. If there's one thing the young Yellowstone area fishery has lacked it is the written tradition, the history of angling in the area.

The Waters of Yellowstone with Rod and Fly is the important first work that begins the written history of fly fishing in the area. This valuable little guidebook lays the foundation upon which other great works have built, and will continue to build the tradition of Yellowstone fly fishing. Howard Back captured the feel, smell, and sounds of the early days of fishing in the Yellowstone country. He developed the mood of angling in Yellowstone, and even now most of the information Back gives us is as current as it was when he wrote it.

My good friend Dan Callaghan, whose knowledge and love for Yellowstone is deep and intimate, once said that "there is more in Yellowstone than just fishing if one will stop, and look, and sense, and feel." His photographs celebrate this idea. Howard Back expressed it best in *Yellowstone Waters with Rod and Fly* when he said that his book was "more than a guidebook in its literal sense. You will find in it something of the imagination as well, for facts without fancy are but dull affairs. You will find a little of the hills and dales, of the flowers and the birds and wild things, of the romance that lies deep in all of us, disguise it how we will."

You should have seen it here in the good ol' days. This often-heard comment regarding most trout waters around the country, and world, is not the case in Yellowstone. The fishing here is as good, and in many cases better, than when Back wrote his book in 1938. We *are* living in the "good ol' days."

There have been many changes in this area since 1938. Howard Back discusses two iron bridges, and a wooden bridge on the Firehole River. Today, one of the iron bridges is concrete and both have been closed to vehicle traffic. The wooden bridge is now concrete. The widow of "Widow's Preserve" has departed and the pond is now called Culver's or Widow's Pond. Fish Lake is known as Trout Lake. Though the list of changes goes on, what is amazing today is how much things have remained the same or have gotten more remote or wild than they were in the 1930s.

Recently, Dan Callaghan and I fished the Madison River below Seven Mile Bridge in the Park. It was here that Back talked about the elk coming down in the evening to water and feed near sentinel rocks along the bank. As on cue, in the early evening the elk came down to the river as I was fishing a Gray Drake spinner fall. He discusses the South Fork of the Madison River and the yellow graveled areas of stream bed; this lovely river, protected through a conservation easement now, is wilder today than in the 1930s, and because of the foresight of today's owners it will never be developed. The planting of inferior hatchery trout has been discontinued. Today few anglers would consider using fly patterns like Jock Scotts for wild trout—though these were touted during Howard Back's time. And after the fires of 1988, Yellowstone country looks different in many places than it did sixty years ago.

Howard Back spent two partial fishing seasons in 1936 and 1937, exploring the waters of Yellowstone. When he talks about the waters of Yellowstone he is referring to not only the waters within the Park but also rivers, lakes, and streams in nearby Idaho, Montana, and Wyoming. His stated purpose in writing his guide was "to record findings and publish it for the benefit of all anglers heading to Yellowstone." He felt that the rivers, lakes, and streams of this area surpassed any water he had fished in the world. He wanted to give fly fishers the nature of the streams, fish types, suggested fly patterns, accommodations, access, and the "lay of the land" so they could avoid wasting time while on their short fishing vacations to Yellowstone. He was a keen observer, nature-lover, and casual fisherman. But he was not thorough. He ignored many important waters in the area that were not pleasing to his temperament, or which are today responsive to modern methods with modern tackle. Nonetheless, Back's honest assessment of the fishery regarding sizes of fish, anglers' expectations, fly patterns, presentation, and more remains mostly accurate to this day. His insights into the future of fishing in Yellowstone Country, with thoughts on catch and release, fly fishing philosophy, education, enforcement, and water quality reveal the farsighted conservationist–fly fisherman that he was.

Twenty-five years ago my wife, Jackie, and I began making a fall trip to Yellowstone to fish, enjoy the Park's scenery and wildlife, and not hear a phone's annoying ring for several weeks. During those early trips we never discussed the notion of moving to the area. But almost unconsciously, with each trip, we fell deeper and deeper in love with this place. Then, one snowy February afternoon while I was tying flies in preparation for our Yellowstone trip, only eight months away, Jackie announced that we were moving to Yellowstone. A few phone calls, a plane flight out to interview for a job, and the purchase of a home sight unseen and over the phone, and we were on our way to paradise.

We agreed to stay two years in Yellowstone. We came to fish, to get to know this "place," and to take in all it had to offer. Then, after our short stay, we'd pack up and head back to the fine jobs, security, and retirement systems we had both left back east. I was the new Police Chief of West Yellowstone, Montana, and Jackie a dispatcher. We left high-paying police positions in Michigan to come to Yellowstone; my salary was less than a thousand dollars a month and Jackie earned less than the minimum wage. The job as "Chief" was so insecure there had been dozens of chiefs in less than two decades. We would feed prisoners in our home because the town then had no money in the prisoners' upkeep budget. I'd often drive my own truck for a patrol vehicle because the town had no money for gasoline. I took care of Presidents and U.S. Secret Servicemen and took them fly fishing in Yellowstone when we had no money for babysitters and Jackie had to take the kids to the police dispatch room-jail when we both worked nights. The girls would run and play through the jail, sleep in the cells, and seldom complain. We were in the "place" called Yellowstone, and we grew as a family to love it and call it our home. After two years, none of us remembered our initial agreement to head back east after our short tenure. We simply did not look back.

Today, after fishing, exploring, and learning about this area for more than thirty years, I realize I can never fish, or know, all of it. Yellowstone National Park alone takes in more country than the states of Delaware, Rhode Island, and the District of Columbia. Within a two-hour drive of West Yellowstone there are more than 2,000 miles of trout streams and hundreds of lakes, ponds, and sloughs; more than 90 percent are open to the public. No area in the world offers more trout water in so contained an area, water so easily accessible as the Yellowstone Country. Howard Back said that there was so much water one need never fish the same water twice in a season.

Recently I fished the Madison River as it flows near the base of National Park Mountain in Yellowstone National Park. Sitting on the bank I watched the water for trout to begin rising to the scheduled evening caddisfly emergence. I could imagine a group of men huddled around a campfire in this tiny meadow in 1870. The men were discussing how they could own and profit from the discoveries that they had just made. One man, Judge Cornelius Hedges of Montana, a member of the Washburn Expedition, came forward and announced that there should be no private ownership of any of this region; rather, the whole of it should be set aside as a National Park. With foresight, these men were able to see the potential of Yellowstone as more than a chance for economic gain. Back felt that everyone who fishes and enjoys our National Parks owes a deep debt of gratitude to the Washburn Expedition of 1870.

Today the fishery in the Yellowstone area is in better shape than when Back wrote his guidebook. The waters are being better managed than those in any other area of the world. The states of Idaho, Montana, and Wyoming, and The Aquatic Resource Center that manages the fishery program in Yellowstone National Park are all responsible for creating innovative programs that not only enhance the area's quality fishery but also protect the environment. The fishing in most of the rivers, lakes, and streams has improved over the past several years and is expected to continue this trend into the future.

Every day I talk to dozens of fly fishers. We'll discuss topics from fly pattern and trout behavior to the philosophy of catch and release and barbless hooks. But the universal issue all anglers want to discuss is the future of their sport. All fly fishers are concerned with what they see for the future of fly fishing. The concerns that Howard back brings up in this book are echoed by today's anglers: increased angling pressure, catch and release philosophy, stream ethics, aggressive enforcement of regulations, education, development along stream corridors, diseases affecting trout, the introduction of exotic species illegally planted in the area waters, and the indiscriminate planting of inferior hatchery trout in waters able to sustain wild populations.

Back's comments on planting hatchery fish in rivers like the Yellowstone in the Park are particularly interesting. Planting trout was widespread in the Park until the 1950s and in Montana until the 1970s. Back felt it was proper to plant trout, "up to, but not beyond the capacity of the water to maintain them." The Yellowstone River from below Yellowstone Lake to the upper falls was regularly planted with cutthroat during Back's time. He reports that the average fish in this section ran around one and a half pounds, roughly the same size as today's trout in this section. Back felt that there were too many fish stocked for the carrying capacity of the river and that the great number of stocked trout kept the average size of the native trout low.

Back regarded his generation of anglers who enjoyed the benefits of public waters as the trustees for the generations to come, and he says that any appeals he makes in his guidebook are made with this belief. He felt that all fly fishers should bring a new spirit and code concerning catch and release and the use of fly fishing over other methods. He insisted on maintaining adequate water levels on Montana's Hebgen Lake; when levels drop below a certain point the fishing season should be closed. Today, fisheries management people in Yellowstone are working in partnerships with power companies, establishing minimum instream flows and protecting wild trout.

According to Back, the number of anglers in the United States was increasing "by leaps and bounds." Since then, the number of fly fishers in the Yellowstone area has increased nearly 500 percent. He felt that the chance to escape the rigors of everyday life and obtain peace by fly fishing in this area must be preserved. Back asks, "What can be done to meet the constant increase in numbers of anglers?" His answer was: "to plant trout to the capacity of the water to maintain them."

We've come a long way in our "wild trout" management programs since then. The fishery has flourished since planting trout in this area was discontinued. No longer must we concern ourselves with the "demand" for more trout in the creel. Now we must take on the issue of whether we will suffocate our trout streams with all the love and attention we crowd upon them. Are the rivers we so love in danger of being loved to death? I am piqued whenever I hear a group of fly fishers discussing their plans to fish a river from 6 AM to 9 PM. The next day they boast of catching and releasing scores of trout. With hooking mortality at 10–15 percent, and many trout in the popular waters being caught and released more than ten times a season, it isn't long before a trout's number comes up, no matter how carefully it is handled and released. All fly fishers love their quarry. There is nothing more lovely than a wild trout. But if we hook, land, touch, photograph, and release as many trout as we can from sun up until dusk, we'll be killing trout unintentionally.

In recent years we have been exploring new country and discovering small streams, beaver ponds, lakes, and hike-in places on major waters that showed little or no angling activity. Back ignored all of these waters; he was on a limited time schedule or they were "not pleasing to his temperament." He maintained there were so many "bests" among Yellowstone waters that the angler need not spend much time exploring or fishing the secondary, off-the-beaten-path waters of Yellowstone Country. Some of these secondary waters are now my favorites. Overlooked streams like the Gardner and Lewis Rivers, tributaries of major streams such as the Taylor's Fork and Specimen Creek of the Gallatin River, and Clear Creek to Yellowstone Lake, lakes like Grizzly, Cascade, and McBride all provide anglers with wonderful opportunities to take wild trout, and, in some cases, grayling.

The final chapter in Howard Back's book is titled, "In Conclusion, and with Some Suggestions." He tiptoed around his constructive suggestions section, calling them delicate issues and fearing they might smack of criticism. He wanted to make helpful and constructive suggestions and offered them only in the interests of good sport and good sportsmanship. He offered his concerns to the angler, and the Federal and State authorities to whom "are entrusted the care of our interests."

Unfortunately, most of the "suggestions" he made sixty years ago are as current and valid now as they were then. If we fail to protect things so important to us—the rivers, wild trout, and wilderness areas—future anglers will have every right to chide us on why we stood around and watched it happen—why we allowed golf courses, gold mines, subdivisions, and grizzly bear zoos to eliminate a wilderness that helps preserve our capacity for wonder, and the power to see and feel the miracles of life: the beauty and the harmony that a place like Yellowstone gives us.

If you love wild trout in the unspoiled waters of Yellowstone you will want to speak more strongly, more clearly, and with more regularity about the concerns affecting our sport. We must work together to find solutions to protect this place we call Yellowstone.

We must join helpful organizations like the Greater Yellowstone Coalition, The Yellowstone Park Foundation, and The Yellowstone Association. We must watch for any slippage of standards.

If Howard Back could see the changes that are happening in Yellowstone today he'd no doubt be pleased. Many roads that had threatened wild trout habitat and animal security areas that were open in his time have been closed or restricted. The trout are wild and no longer planted, wilderness areas have been established, and catch and release fishing is being practiced by nearly all anglers fishing this wonderland. Outside the park thousands of acres of wildlife and prime trout habitat have been protected by ranchers and other land owners placing their properties into conservation easements, a program that forever protects environmentally sensitive lands from subdivision and harmful development. The Yellowstone area's great diversity of pristine, pure waters is in fine shape, and the future looks fine. We all agree on our love of wild trout, unspoiled wilderness, and a place called Yellowstone. Let's all work in partnership to preserve the heritage her waters have given us—past, present, and future.

These organizations support and fund projects enhancing your Yellowstone fishing experience. Howard Back would encourage your support of them.

The Yellowstone Park Foundation
37 East Main, Suite 4
Bozeman, MT 59715

The Yellowstone Association
Box 117
Yellowstone National Park, WY 82190

Greater Yellowstone Coalition
Box 1874
Bozeman, MT 59771

CRAIG MATHEWS
West Yellowstone, Montana

THE WATERS OF YELLOWSTONE

With Rod and Fly

CHAPTER ONE

APOLOGIA PRO LIBRO MEO

IT has become almost traditional for the author of a new book about angling to preface his work with an apology for adding to the already vast number of books bearing upon that subject. Personally I do not think that any such apology is needed. The more the merrier, say I. I read them all, or all of which I become aware; for surely the next best thing to going fishing oneself is to go fireside fishing with a fellow angler. However, if it be the correct thing to do, I will by way of apology explain the origin and purpose of this modest volume.

Let me state from the outset that I have no thought or pretension of entering the lists with the great pen-men of angling. I am not about to propound any new theories, whether about the habits of fish, the methods employed to catch them, the tying of flies or the construction of rods or reels or any other of the *engins de pêche*. I am, alas, still at the bottom of the second class as an angler (and even at that I may be over-estimating myself!); and, I blush to admit it, but you will soon find it out, I am in no class at all as an author. I do, however, claim to be at the top of the first class as an angling enthusiast, and in that capacity I have a story to tell to the American angling fraternity which, so far as I

can ascertain, has not been told before. It is a story
both of interest and of usefulness, and it is also, as you
shall see, a story with a moral. It should be told by
someone combining the profound knowledge of a
Hewitt, a Skues or a La Branche with the literary skill
of a Plunket Greene, a Romilly Fedden or a Patrick
Chalmers (Patrick "Charmer" he is to me). Since, however, no such paragon has come forth to tell the story
of this anglers' paradise, I have set myself the task of
blazing the trail, hoping that some day someone better
equipped than myself will write it as it should be
written. The subject matter is well worthy of first-
class authorship. I have had the advantage of a varied
and extensive fishing experience, both in Europe and
on this continent; yet I can say with conviction that,
for all-round merit as a trout-fishing area, the waters
in and around Yellowstone Park surpass any waters
that I know, not excluding those of the Salzkammergut
of Austria.

And yet if you, Sir, were one fine day to say to yourself, "I think I will take a holiday and go fishing in
Yellowstone for a week or two; I must look up some
books about it," you would then and there find yourself checkmated, for up to date no succinct work of information upon that subject is available, so far as I have
been able to ascertain. When in 1936 I decided to go
and see something of the Western States, I put out
feelers for information on the angling possibilities of
Yellowstone. In the Anglers' Club of New York I was
not lucky enough to locate anyone who had been so

far afield except Jack McCloy. Despite the pressure which is always upon the shoulders of a successful attorney, Jack found time to write me several pages on his experiences on the Madison and the Gallatin. Nowhere else amongst my small circle of acquaintances could I find any contributors either of direct knowledge or book knowledge. I did learn from a friend in Houston of the almost mythical existence of the Widow's Preserve somewhere up in the hills of Montana, of which you shall hear more anon; but that, at the time, could hardly be classified as knowledge. When I reached Yellowstone I wasted interminable and priceless hours in seeking out the truth. I made all the mistakes of the stranger. I found only the obvious waters. In the short time at my then disposal, however, I saw enough to realize the wonders of the place. Then and there I made up my mind that, if at all possible, I would return in 1937 and get to know Yellowstone; that I might even make a record of my findings and publish it for the benefit of any angler who might find himself in the same predicament.

That, then, is the origin of this book. Mind you, when I speak of information I mean the kind of information which a serious angler requires when he sets out to a distant and somewhat isolated spot for a vacation of limited duration. What does he require? Not the generic and picturesque nonsense compiled for pamphlets by publicity departments about "speckled beauties" and "the thrill of the leaping captive," but some reasonably sound but simple first-hand knowl-

edge compiled by an angler for the benefit of anglers—
the nature of the streams and lakes which he will encounter, the types of fish to be found in them, the flies
and kit which will be most appropriate, where best to
find accommodation, and above all clear indications,
with plans if possible, of methods of access to the waters,
so that he can, without waste of time, find his way
quickly and expeditiously to the riverside. I know
of no greater tragedy than the time which has often
to be wasted by a keen angler on a short vacation in
finding out the "lay of the land." It is largely in order
to prevent that tragedy from occurring to others who
wish to fish in and around Yellowstone that I have
written this book.

So, you see, I am in some sense tendering to the
angling public a guide-book to these waters, or rather
to such of them as I have been able to cover in the all
too short time at my disposal. Unfortunately, like the
majority of anglers, I have to earn my modest livelihood
elsewhere and otherhow; yet I did manage to put in
some six weeks of study before having the effrontery
to compile this work. I stayed in West Yellowstone
from June 24th to July 21st and again from August
7th to 24th. I purposely wished to see the waters at
their worst, which is in the last week of July and the
first half of August. I only wish I could have seen them
at their best in early June or in September. Later in
this book you will learn the reason for these periodic
variations in the quality of the fishing. To do this work
justice the author should have known the rivers in all

their phases.

Rivers, as you know, change unaccountably in character, and even in appearance, from week to week and from month to month. You surely have had the experience of returning to a stream for a renewed acquaintanceship only to find it somehow changed, somehow different, so that you have said to yourself, "Can this be the same stream that I fished but a year ago?" Sometimes the change is definable in cause or character; at other times it is intangible; but the change is there, and for once the change is not in you. When you go back, after the years, to the old school, to find that the campus, which to boyhood's eyes seemed immense, a world in itself, is but a little plot of acres, it is you, my friend, who have changed, and not the campus. But when you return to a river, which you have loved in some other year or at some other time of year, only to find it all different, the change will be in the river and its ways, and not in you. A hundred and one causes may have been at work, causes too long to list at this writing. I make this point in self-defence against possible future criticism. I have told of things as I have actually seen them during the weeks I was in Yellowstone. To do this work justice I should have stayed beside the waters from the spring snow-melt until the re-blanketing in the fall. You know the old travel story: "What city is this, my dear?" "I don't know, my love. What day is it?" "Tuesday the twenty-fourth." "Then it must be Venice." That illustrates just about how ignorant I still feel about this land of bright waters.

And yet I think I can fairly claim that by early rising and forced marches I have managed to cover so much ground that a careful perusal of these notes will enable any conscientious angler to derive the maximum of enjoyment, with the minimum of time wasted, out of a stay in Yellowstone. So much water is there for him to fish that in the length of a normal vacation he need never fish the same water twice. That he will do so, if he be a true angler, is certain; for there will be favourite stretches, corners of particular appeal, to which he will return again and again. He will suffer from embarrassment of riches. His daily choice of a venue will be a heart-searching affair. For me, personally, there was a bounden duty, which I owed to my conscience, to cover as much ground, or rather as much water, as possible; for how could I write about water which I had never fished, or even seen? I shudder, or rather I perspire, to think how many miles I tramped in the summer of 1937 in order to be thus at peace with my conscience. Yet they were happy miles, every yard of them. I hope that some day I may tramp them all over again. I would hate to tell you how often I have had to stamp out the fire of insurrection within me as I have started out at daybreak in some new direction, when there was some particular and beloved stretch of river calling me back to have another try at that big fellow under the willows which broke me a few days back.

I have explained, then, how in a sense this work is a guide-book to the principal angling waters of Yellow-

*I did learn from a friend in Houston of the almost mythical existence of the
Widow's Preserve somewhere up in the Hills of Montana . . .*

You will find a little of the hills and dales, of the flowers and the birds and the wild things, of the romance that lies deep in all of us, disguise it how we will. For is it not of all these things that the true meaning of that wonder word "angling" is made up?

stone. That is true, and yet it is more than a guide-book in its literal sense. You will find in it something of the imagination as well, for facts without fancy are but dull affairs. You will find a little of the hills and dales, of the flowers and the birds and the wild things, of the romance that lies deep in all of us, disguise it how we will. For is it not of all these things that the true meaning of that wonder word "angling" is made up? No man can give the best that is in him if he attempt to suppress a vital part of his true self, that self which is made up of the web of life's experiences. I happen to have witnessed at first hand through two weary years the horrors of modern warfare. I have watched the birth of a new world. It was to have been a world "fit for heroes to live in"; it is, what?—a world of greed and cruelty as never before, a world wherein the promise of the strong to defend the weak is as a broken pitcher, where honour between nations is overruled by expediency, a world wherein whole suffering peoples are subjected to the baneful mesmerism of egotistical "leaders" who are hurrying their subjects to death and destruction, "leaders" whom the Gods have long since made mad but have as yet failed to destroy. I have learned that, if blood be thicker than water, money is thicker than blood; and, finally, I have lost the one wonderful person whose unbounded loyalty and uprightness made full compensation for all of life's bitter deceptions. Therefore I have formed, in self-defence, a habit of make-believe without which I do not think I would care to face whatever of the road still lies before me. It may creep into my task, whether I will or no, for I have been unable to live in the beauty of Yellowstone without feeling the touch of fairies' wings as they flitted from flower to flower. Therefore if, in describing these waters, I have added some fancy to my facts, if here and there I have, as it were, mixed a little Barrie with my Baedeker, I tender this explanation and apology and pray you to accept me as I am.

Finally, in order that you may have some foresight of the promised land, I have done my beginner's best with a camera. No picture can do justice to the loveliness of these running waters, flowered valleys and watching hills. Yet I hope that the Publisher (if indeed I succeed in finding one) will agree to the inclusion of some of these pictures, for somehow a book about angling particularly favours the reproduction of scenes from actual life.

And so to my story. It is a story that I have lived with all the enthusiasm which only an angler knows. In writing it I shall be living over happy hours again. I can only hope that it will awake in the hearts of some of my fellow anglers a desire to follow in my footsteps, and to know and enjoy the beautiful places which are theirs.

CHAPTER TWO

ABOUT YELLOWSTONE PARK

I WISH to make it clear that in speaking of Yellowstone I am not referring solely to the Yellowstone National Park, but to the Park and the surrounding country, and in particular the country lying to its west. I have been guided in my wanderings by the merits of various rivers, as I judge them, and not by any geographical consideration of State boundaries, Park lines or other conventional delimitations of area. If, therefore, you "come fishing with me" you will be wetting your line in waters under the jurisdiction sometimes of the National Park Services, other times of the States of Wyoming, Montana and Idaho. When you fish within Yellowstone Park, which lies mostly in Wyoming but partly also in Montana and Idaho, no licence will be required of you. You will be asked to pay three dollars, for the right to come and go with your car in the Park for the current year, to refrain from killing any living thing save fish (and only a limited number of those per day), and to respect a few reasonable and proper regulations drawn up for the protection of both man and beast. If you fish outside the Park line you must then be armed with a licence to fish in the State in which you find yourself, be it Wyoming, Montana or Idaho. If you follow me, it

9

will mostly be in Montana, the annual out-of-state licence for which is $3.50 for the season.

At this point let me say a few words about the Yellowstone National Park for the benefit of those who have not studied the history of our National Parks, which come under the authority of the Ministry of the Interior. For you will be spending much of your time in a National Park and you will owe much of your pleasure to the foresight of those who founded the Park and to the efficiency of the National Park Services which maintain it.

The National Parks are essentially "sanctuaries." They are non-commercially operated, in contradistinction to the National Forests. No gun may be fired within their boundaries, no warm-blooded animal killed, no flower, shrub or tree picked or destroyed. The only living things which may be killed, except by special authority, are fish, and those are bred and fed for the slaughter in countless thousands.

Locally the Park is under the charge of a Superintendent, aided by a Chief Ranger in charge of the Ranger service. There are about 31 permanent Rangers in Yellowstone Park. In order that you may appreciate these men at their true worth, I recommend you to read a book entitled *Oh, Ranger!* It is written by Horace Albright and Frank Taylor and published by Dodd, Mead and Co. It tells you all about the lives of the Rangers—their winter life, hemmed in by the snows and subsisting on canned food laid in before winter sets in, responsible for the care of all the denizens of the forest; their summer life, hemmed in by tourists, and responsible for them too. Ask any Ranger which of the two, tourist or wild animal, is the more capable of taking care of himself! They are all picked men, these Rangers, nature lovers, happier to shoot with a camera than with a gun, fearless woodsmen, keen anglers and good sportsmen. They are responsible for the safety, order and welfare of the Park and all within its boundaries. Forest fires are their particular care, for a serious forest fire may ruin large tracts of this vast holiday land for a generation and more. Lightning is responsible for some fires, carelessness for others. I can only express a hope that no angler who reads this book will ever have that crime upon his conscience.

They are busy men, this band of thirty odd, for in the summer some half million tourists and sportsmen visit Yellowstone Park. In order to help cope with this ever-increasing influx, temporary Rangers are drafted in for the summer period, "Ninety Day Wonders" as they are facetiously called, clean-cut lads, some of whom so take to the life that they adopt it professionally and become permanent Rangers. Bear this distinction in mind and do not expect technical angling information from a temporary Ranger. I say this in no disparagement; it is not his province. Get, if you can, to know a permanent Ranger, and then you will find things out, many things probably which I have missed. For they live with the rivers year in, year out; they know the trails; they find out the hidden places which are good to know; and, if they sum you up as a good sportsman, they will unburden their knowledge to you. I wish I had realized this back in 1936.

Oh, Ranger! will tell you all about bears and other animals, and a little about fishing. A word about bears. You will read notices, *passim* in the Park, warning you against the danger of feeding bears. Most of the time all goes well with bear feeders, but every now and then an accident happens, and then it is too late for regrets. Bears, after all, are wild beasts and, despite the tameness which "sanctuary" has instilled in them, they are yet capable at any moment, and for no very obvious reason, of reverting to type. I confess that on one occasion I tactfully retired in the face of an oncoming bear of enormous bulk and mean aspect. I even abandoned my favourite Payne rod, which I was in process of dismounting and which happily I recovered later unharmed. I was taking no chances.

Of course on the other side of the picture there is the old story of the wood-cutter, which makes up in humour what it lacks in gallantry. The scene is laid by the wood-cutter's cottage in the forest, from which, through a clearing, the distant village may be seen. As the good man is plying his ax, up runs his little daughter, white faced and calling "Daddy, Daddy!" "What is it, my dear?" asks the good man. "Mummy is on her way back from the village," replies the child, "I can see her through the clearing, and behind a tree I can see a great big bear waiting for her. What shall we do?" The wood-cutter pauses awhile, then gravely replies: "Darling, we can do nothing at all about it.

That bear has got into its own mess, and it must get out of it the best way it can." But seriously, my advice to you on the whole is to leave bears alone.

You will read in *Oh, Ranger!* how it was at the junction of the Firehole and Gibbon rivers, where now is Madison Junction, that the National Park idea was born around the camp-fire of the Washburn-Langford Expedition. Hence Yellowstone is the mother of all National Parks. It is difficult to exaggerate what a wonderful sanctuary for animals and playground for humans this Park is, or what a debt of gratitude is owed by all Americans to those who had the vision to set it aside for perpetual peace and enjoyment. Think of it—more than 3,400 square miles of rivers, mountains and valleys where peace reigns in this world of turmoil, where no gun may be shot, no law of kindness violated.

You must purchase the excellent guide-book to the Park by Jack Haynes. It is fat with information, well and clearly drawn up and indexed. You will now and then want to give your casting arm a rest; otherwise your timing will become stale and lose its fine edge. On those "off" days you will do well to follow Mr. Haynes. You will find in him a sure guide. He will take you to geysers varying in size from a wash-basin to a pond. He will explain to you what makes a geyser geyse, and how a beaver beaves—I mean behaves. In fact he opens the door to all general knowledge concerning the Park. With regard to fishing, his information is admittedly limited; he only tells you what fish are to be found in what rivers; but then you are not fishing with him; you are sightseeing with him, but fishing, I hope, with me.

If you like geysers you may have your fill of them. Their acrid odour to me is distasteful, but some of the pools, like Emerald and Morning Glory, are of extreme beauty and should not be missed. Old Faithful is, of course, by far the most imposing, but for some reason which I am unable to explain I find myself irritated by its clocklike precision and punctuality. Whenever I see it "go up," I find myself wishing that one fine day it would get "off centre" and play truant, going off early or late or not at all. There is something inartistic in its set regularity. I can see the face of the lecturing Ranger as he eyes his wrist-watch in dismay and mutters to himself, "What, no eruption?"

In point of fact a Ranger friend tells me that he once did see Old Faithful run over its time; he waited fifteen minutes and even then nothing happened. My congratulations to the old geyser for once having been "Unfaithful"; or should I say with the poet "Falsely True"?

If flowers be your passion (and if you visit Yellowstone in June they must surely become your passion) you will find in any of the Haynes Picture Shops *Trees and Flowers of Yellowstone National Park,* by Frank Thone, with sketches by Margaret Thone, a simple and excellent work by which you can identify your favourites. If you like colour plates, *Flowers of Mountain and Plain,* by Edith Clements, will fill your bill.

If you like geysers you may have your fill of them. Their acrid odour to me is distasteful, but some of the pools, like Emerald and Morning Glory, are of extreme beauty and should not be missed.

The elk bellow and bugle and look majestic.

It is impossible to exaggerate the beauty of the wild flowers in June. They carpet the river banks in a riot of colour—reds, yellows and blues prevailing. They demand your appreciation. You will find yourself mentally selecting your favourites. Perhaps the crimson of the Indian paint brush will win your heart with its almost unnatural vividness. If delicacy and rarity are winning points, then the Mariposa lily may become your love.

For me the little white phlox, with its waxen white flowers pinned flat onto its cushion of green, modestly turning the earth into an inverted sky, makes special appeal, sharing equal honours with the delicate blue harebell, playing chimes in the breeze, and taking me back over the gulf of the years to the shores of Loch Ness where I first saw it and loved it in the golden age. Lupin and larkspur, musk and forget-me-not, primrose and flax, spurge, mallow, geranium, wild rose, foxglove, columbine tricked out in all the colours of the pantomime, blue, red, gold and white, they still dance before me—all those and many more too numerous to mention.

And when all the early pageant has passed by, and the river banks begin to look bare, nature has still a surprise in store. Slowly at first, just here and there, and then in ever-increasing quantities and larger and brighter patches, the gentians burst upon an unsuspecting world, turning the very atmosphere into royal blue, a sight that must be seen to be believed.

Once, and once only, have I seen mass effect to equal

it, at Manor Lake near Bay City in Texas. I had gone as Hal Houseman's guest for an overnight stay, to fish for the black bass with which these waters abound. On the evening of our arrival we fished the smaller lake, and after supper sat watching the alligators come up to feed, their eyes shining bright red in the glow of our torches, an eerie sight. I remember promising myself to keep well seated in the boat on the morrow! Before dawn we were away on the big lake, each in his own craft with a coloured boy to pole him. Out through the tropical swamp we slipped and over acres of lily pads into the more open water. Dotted all over were countless small islets of high reeds and vegetation, just visible in the tail end of the night.

As I commenced to fish, the first rays of the sun broke in the sky. First came a twitter from a near-by island; then a squawk. Then up came the sun with a sudden glow of warmth. As at a signal, thousands upon thousands of birds awoke and burst into a pæan of praise, birds of all colours and types, a very orchestra of feathered players. It was just then that I saw it—all around me, as far as the eye could reach, not thousands, not tens of thousands, but hundreds and hundreds of thousands of lily buds burst open, as at a word of command, and spread their waxen white glory to greet the opening day, great white globes with golden centres, gently opening and stretching their limbs, "pure from the night and splendid for the day," acre upon waxen acre of them. Never did I witness a more beautiful salute to Dawn.

Of snakes you will see none in this wonder-land—not venomous ones, at least. You may on the Bechler River or Slough Creek come across a grass snake or two, but you may rest assured that they are harmless. To me —who live and fish in Texas, where rattlesnakes and moccasins abound and where, when fishing, I walk like Agag, always a little distracted by the unpleasant possibility of attack—the relief of being able to watch the running water without fear of where I plant my feet is unspeakable.

Then the birds; you can imagine how they revel in the unmolested peace of the place. Somewhere I have read a work on the Birds of Yellowstone, published, if memory serves me aright, under the auspices of the Roosevelt Wild Life Forest Experiment Station, whose centre is Syracuse University. It is most informative and contains many reproductions of excellent photographs. I have no knowledge of American bird life, which for the most part varies considerably from the European. There seems to me to be a greater range of colouration in American birds. In the smaller birds, bright red, blue and yellow types abound. One which I watched, spell-bound, for half an hour, on the Bechler River, was a combination of black and pale and dark yellows. "Oranges and Lemons" I called him. Bluebirds abound, as do also kingfishers and jays. The hawk family, of course, is in its element. One nest I found of a member of that family, the Night Hawk, or Night Jar as it is called in England. "Nest" is, perhaps, an inappropriate word, for it makes no nest, just lays its two mottled eggs on the bare ground.

The first one I ever saw was found by a schoolmate with whom I was egg hunting on Hazeley Heath, Winchfield, more years ago than I care to tell. I swopped in my best cricket bat for one of the pair. It must have been a prophetic act, for later, when I went to Marlborough College, I was excused from cricket in order that I might study natural history, for which I had a special bent. That was a rare privilege in an English "public school," where cricket, which seemed to me a dull pursuit, is part of the religion of one's up-bringing.

On the Madison, one evening, a little below the iron bridge, I saw a white egret. I gathered later from Ranger Chapman that they are not often seen in that section of the Park. It had no mate that I could see. I used to watch them in thousands in the Egyptian Delta where I have spent no small part of my life. At one time they came in danger of extinction; they were saved by a timely enactment of Lord Kitchener order-ing their protection.

I think that next to fish the birds are the most im-portant element in a day's angling. They are so varied and so fascinating to watch. If you agree with me you will find Yellowstone teeming with interest, for the variety of the birds is boundless and their tameness remarkable.

If you get "Parkitis" badly, there is one other book, of course, which you will procure and read. It is en-titled *The Yellowstone National Park* and is written

The buffalo and moose look exotic and dangerous.

The woodchuck chirrups at you from some coign of advantage.

by General Chittenden who for many years was in charge of all engineering works in the Park. It is the outstanding and authoritative classic upon the subject.

Now, having paid a very proper tribute to the founders of the Park, to its management, to its bibliographers and to its flora and fauna, let us come a little nearer to its most neglected inhabitants, the trout and grayling—neglected, that is, in story and song, but by no means neglected in cultivation and in capture. I suppose that their invisibility is the principal cause of that neglect. The bears come out into the roadway and positively hold you up for contributions. The elk bellow and bugle and look majestic. The buffalo and moose look exotic and dangerous. The beaver, when you can catch sight of him, looks a picture of industry. The woodchuck chirrups at you from some coign of advantage. The birds flit from tree to tree, blue, red, yellow, splashes of colour from nature's generous palette. All of them are visible, catching your eye and ear, lending to the feeling of one vast happy family within the boundaries of this chosen land.

Only the fish remain unseen, unheard. But for the occasional dart of a kingfisher, or the dive of an osprey, you might fail to suspect their presence. Yet there they are in their thousands and tens of thousands, as beautiful of garb as any other denizen of the Park, as lithe and agile, as wonderful in mechanism and instinct, populating the running waters and the depths of the lakes, waiting to give you thrill upon thrill, the thrill of sudden contact with an unknown, unseen, quarry, the thrill which sets your heart a-bumping in your throat and your knees a-quaking in your waders. They alone of all living things in the Park pay the penalty for the benefit of your pleasure. So when later in this book I beg you to be a good sportsman in return, think of them, please, as worthy of your appreciation and sportsmanship.

CHAPTER THREE

ABOUT TYPES OF FISH

I NOW propose to tell you what types of fish are to be found in the Yellowstone area and how they come to be there. You will angle the more intelligently if you are well informed as to the nature, character and "provenance" of your quarry.

First let me recommend you to acquire from the Bureau of Fisheries in Washington a publication entitled *Fishes of the Yellowstone National Park*. It was compiled by Hugh Smith and William Kendall and published in 1921. That pamphlet tells you the history of the indigenous fishes and the introduced fishes; it also summarizes the origins and runs of all the rivers.

In case you cannot, or do not, procure it, and in order that the present work may in any event be reasonably complete in itself, I propose to give you a list of the sporting fish which you will encounter, together with some information on spawning times, habits, propagation and hatcheries. I have visited all the hatcheries in and around the Park, and many much further afield. Even, however, were I sufficiently informed to enter safely into the deeper technicalities of the subject of trout classification, I propose to reduce this part of my work to the simplest possible terms. Personally I hold the belief that there **is a** tendency to catalogue under separate species some variations of trout which are really one and the same species, whose variations from type are due to special conditions appertaining to the locality in which they live. That problem need not concern you, but if it does interest you I recommend you to read *A History of Fishes,* by J. R. Norman (Ernest Benn, Ltd., London), Chapter XVIII, on "Classification." It is a book full of interest in any event, and written by a great authority.

To begin with, you have in the Yellowstone area two indigenous game fishes, *salmo lewisi* and *salmo thymallus montanus.* I do not propose to count the whitefish, *coregonus williamsoni,* as a game fish.

Salmo lewisi

This may be said to be the Yellowstone fish "par excellence." It is colloquially known as blackspotted or native. It is also known as cutthroat, owing to the two coral red slashes under its throat. The word "native" comes easier to hand, but I avoid it because to those who live in the East the word "native" has become synonymous with the Eastern brook trout, whereas the word cutthroat has no other application that I know of, outside of three handed bridge! I therefore propose throughout this work to refer to it as the cutthroat.

The cutthroat is a first-class sporting fish. It takes the fly with avidity and plays well whilst the play lasts. It has not a very prolonged power of fight, and the battle, once over, is definitely over, with none of those surprise recoveries to which the rainbow often treats you. It has now been planted and flourishes in various waters in the Park and throughout the West, but Yellowstone Lake and River are still its big stamping ground and are confined solely to it. It is in Yellowstone Lake that the big capital stock of these fish lives and thrives, and from there that they ascend the various tributaries to carry out the annual process of propagation.

The cutthroat is a spring spawner, spring in Yellowstone meaning approximately June; for the ice and snow do not begin to melt until the latter part of May. Directly the urge seizes them, up they go and seek the shallow waters of the tributaries, large and small, but the smaller ones for preference. It is a source of perpetual amazement to me up what a tiny rivulet a gravid fish will make its way to spawn. They always go up-stream, or so I believe. I do not fancy that any fish run northward out of the lake down the Yellowstone River to spawn. All the fish that you will catch north of the lake are, I believe, fish which have been planted there, or fish which have been locally bred from planted fish.

It is at this spawning stage that the hand of man plays a part in the game, a part without which many an angler would go home disgruntled at his lack of sport. For if the fish were permitted to spawn naturally, the major portion of their eggs would fall a prey to the numerous enemies that lie in wait. Therefore the fish are trapped as they run up-stream and stripped of a large part of their spawn, which is then hatched out under inspection in Federal and State hatcheries. The fish, after being stripped, are put back in the river and continue on up-stream to complete the natural process and evacuate the balance of eggs and milt that are left in them.

I said "hatched out." This hatching is done in two stages. In the local hatchery the eggs are ripened until they reach the stage known as "eyed ova," which means that through the transparent skin of the egg you can perceive the black spot of the embryo fish's developed eye. At this stage they are dispatched to "feeding hatcheries," where they are brought to full development. They are then and from there redistributed as fry, under the direction of the Bureau of Fisheries, to the points where they are most needed.

The hatchery at Lake Junction on Yellowstone Lake confines itself to the stripping of cutthroat trout, and large demands for these fish are satisfied from this origin. The Park, in return for supplying the eyed ova, has a first call on the hatched fish to the extent of its own requirements. The Lake Junction hatchery, which is open to the public, and which you certainly ought to visit, is fed from traps on eleven different streams which run into the lake. In 1937 an all-time record—in fact a world record—for one hatchery was set. No less than forty million eyed ova were handled and passed out in good condition to the feeding hatcheries, almost one hundred per cent arriving in a perfect state at their destination, so skilled is the work of dispatch. In these days we are becoming accustomed to "astronomical figures" but I confess that my mind boggles at the thought of forty million trout!

Despite the punishment which the cutthroats take every summer, the head of fish in the lake keeps at better than parity, the evidence of the traps being that it is steadily increasing. The size of the fish, however, is in my opinion disappointingly small. This may be the penalty which we pay for interfering in a benevolent manner with Dame Nature; perhaps she intended that the major part of the spawn should fall by the wayside. I believe that some good-sized fish are caught in the lake, particularly around Stevenson Island; but in the Yellowstone River I have caught many, yet not one above two pounds in weight. Even in the lake they are to my mind disappointingly small. I am told that in the traps a four-pound fish is unusual and considered big. Of course in the river—that is, the north river running out of the lake which is the only section of the river reasonably accessible to the public —the size may be explained by my supposition that no fish come down-stream out of the lake.

If this be admitted, then the fish which the anglers catch are planted fish, and the question arises in one's mind, "Are too many fish planted in proportion to the food content in this section of the river?" It may of course be that there are big fish but they do not get caught. I doubt, however, if that is the answer, for I have watched dozens of catches, yet nary as good as a two-pounder amongst them.

A more likely explanation, perhaps, is that the planted fish, when ripe for spawning, rarely spawn in the river or its creeks but run on up through the lake to spawn with their brothers and sisters of the lake in the up-stream tributaries, and never return below the lake again. If this be assumed, then there would always be left in the river below the lake the young semi-mature fish, and the problem of size would be accounted for. Yet the lake fish and the trapped fish are small too. A water like Yellowstone Lake ought surely to turn out quite a few fish up to ten pounds. Hence my own feeling is that in all probability the head of fish is too heavy for the food content of the water, both in the lake and in the river.

In Henry's Lake, a few miles west of the Park, the cutthroats run much larger than in Yellowstone. One of over ten pounds was caught this year by the hatchery men. They attributed the difference, in a conversation which I had with them, to the difference in water temperature, the Yellowstone water being very much colder. Cold water, they contend, tends to keep the fish small. I don't believe a word of it. I hold that it is all a matter of feed.

It may of course be argued that the need for a large breeding stock to supply all requirements is so great that size must be sacrificed to quantity. Again, as regards the river, it may be argued that the tourists come in their thousands to catch fish; that the Yellowstone

River is the easiest and most accessible river for them, so it is stuffed full of fish for their amusement and in order that things shall be made easy for them. Better they should catch a few small fish than very occasional big ones. Either of these may be the explanation, and a perfectly justifiable one in the eyes of a paternal department. To me it is a problem which interests technically, and I should like to know the answer.

I made a reference earlier in this book to the name of Plunket Greene. Harry Plunket Greene, who was a singer by profession, and beloved of all who knew him (he but recently passed away), wrote one of the most beautiful books of angling ever penned, entitled *Where the Bright Waters Meet*. It is, in the main, the tale of a little Hampshire chalk stream, called the Bourne, a tributary of the famous Test, into which it runs at the Heronry. I have fished it many a happy time. The book tells of the great days of that little river and the giant fish which were caught year after year by the syndicate of sportsmen who leased it, of whom Plunket Greene for a time was one. It goes on to relate how in course of time the lessees became ambitious; how, not content with what the Gods so generously provided, they decided to increase their stock of great fish. So they stocked the little Bourne beyond its capacity to nourish adequately its new inhabitants. The result was tragedy. Nature took offence. Every effort to repair the damage failed, and for years the river ceased to be fishworthy. I cite this partly for the pleasure of advising my readers of a great angling classic, in case its existence has never come to their knowledge (and if it has I know they will agree with me and forgive my redundant advice), and partly to explain that from this so well told lesson I have learned, where fish are unexplainably small, to suspect over-stocking.

Before closing my paragraph on the cutthroat I must add that to my palate it is by far the most delicious of the fresh water trout family on the breakfast or dinner table. To me it has something of the taste of a grilse, together with an absence of muddiness which is prevalent in most fresh water trout. I have only eaten them out of the Yellowstone River itself. It may be that this particular river holds some crustacean or other food matter which gives them this peculiar delicacy of flavour. I know that I often wish I could conjure one down here on to my Texas dinner table.

One other curious attribute I have noticed. The cutthroat, when killed and cleaned, does not stiffen up like any other trout but remains peculiarly soft, almost flaccid to the touch. I do not know the reason for this; possibly its scales are finer than those of the other varieties, either in texture or in size.

So much for our first indigenous fish, *salmo lewisi*, or the cutthroat.

Salmo thymallus montanus

Our other indigenous fish is the grayling. He too is a spring spawning fish, and what I have explained about the process of propagation for the cutthroat applies also to all the other fish of which I shall speak, including the grayling, but excluding the mackinaw. They all run up from the lakes to the minor tributaries to spawn. There they are trapped, partially stripped, and returned to the water to complete the balance of the process in the natural way. The central depot, as it were, for the grayling in the Park is Grebe Lake. This is a comparatively small lake but abounds in food and produces fine fish and fine fishing. It is generally opened to fishing in the latter part of August. In addition to its grayling it holds some very large and sporting rainbows.

The grayling is a salmonid, having the adipose fin distinctive of that genus. It is named *thymallus* on account of its peculiar odour, like thyme. It requires, in order to thrive, very pure, clear, and preferably fast water. For the angler it is an easy fish, in this country at least. It is exceptionally quick in action. It is able to rise and sink in the water with amazing swiftness. It has the same general construction as the European grayling, with its large sail-like dorsal fin, though in the American cousin the markings in that fin are more beautifully marbled and coloured than in the European.

When I say that it is an easy fish, I mean that, when on the feed, it will come and come again, even when badly pricked. At times it seems determined to get caught. The European grayling, on the contrary, when put down stays down. The grayling may be fished wet or dry with equal success.

The greatest grayling day I ever enjoyed was some years back on the river Wertoch in Bavaria, as a guest of my good friend Millian Trinks. He and I each took one of his twin daughters as a gillie. Evy and I recorded just under fifty grayling on the dry fly before 2 P. M. The few which we retained we split and grilled on Fire Island, as the twins named it. Ever since that day I have regarded a fresh caught grayling as a delicacy. The finest grayling I know of are to be caught on the river Traun at Gmunden in the Salzkammergut, but the Yellowstone grayling run them very close. In one respect the Montana grayling is superior. When hooked it jumps repeatedly and often successfully. When I caught my first grayling in the South Fork I was completely misled by the immediate series of leaps which followed the strike.

I have not found the grayling to be very numerous, nor have I caught a single one in the Madison River. Probably their "easiness" causes them to be taken out sooner than the trout. To me the chance of an occasional grayling lends added charm to a day's angling. "With here and there a lusty trout and here and there a grayling," I recall, but from what poem I no longer remember.

The Introduced Fishes

We now come to the introduced fishes, which are five in number: *salmo levenensis,* or Loch Leven; *salmo fario,* or brown trout, often referred to as German brown; *salmo shasta,* or rainbow; *salvelinus fontinalis* or Eastern brook trout, which is in reality a char; and *cristivomer namaycush* or lake trout, often referred to as the mackinaw.

Salmo levenensis and salmo fario

The first two of this category, *levenensis* and *fario,* I am going, for simplicity's sake, to class as one, and refer to as browns. My reason for this simplification is twofold; they are both fall spawners, and they are so alike in character and appearance that even the trappers will admit that for the most part they cannot differentiate between them. By my reasoning *levenensis* is a local variation of *fario,* due to some peculiar condition prevailing in Loch Leven. Be that as it may, the word brown comes easily to the pen and to the tongue, so I have preferred it to Loch Leven as a generic title.

It is, of course, inevitable that crossing between the two types takes place all the time in these waters, so that in a period of years from first introduction there will probably be created by fusion a new type, German Lochs or brown Levens, call them what you will. Probably some day some ingenious species divider will invent the new species, *salmo hebgenensis!* I shall then claim prior art!

The supply of these fish in the Grayling, Duck, South Fork and Madison, and via the Madison in the lower waters of the Gibbon and Firehole rivers, runs up automatically from Hebgen Lake, to which water considerable reference will be made later in this work. The quantity required for planting in the Park is therefore small. In the case of the Gibbon, the Firehole and the Grayling rivers a certain amount of planting has to be done in the upper waters, since in each case there are falls over which running fish either cannot, or are not likely to, pass. None are planted in the Yellowstone River, which, as I have stated, is preserved for the cutthroats.

There are three stripping stations for browns under the control of the Montana State authorities, on the Madison, Duck and South Fork rivers respectively. That on the South Fork has only just been initiated. At these traps both spring and fall fish are taken up and stripped; they are not used for trapping browns alone.

The Park authorities control, I believe, a brown stripping station on Meadow Lake outside the Park.

The brown trout and his qualities are known to most anglers in this country, in which he is widely spread. He is more adaptable to wide distribution than any other variety, since he is not averse to the less cold waters of some parts of the continent. In the Yellowstone area he is somewhat inconsistent in behaviour, more so than any other variety in my experience. I have caught browns that gave but poor sport; yet on July 7th, about a mile above Baker's Hole, I hooked a fish that played like a four-pounder. It took me over twenty minutes to bring it to the surface and when I

It is colloquially known as blackspotted or native. It is also known as cut-throat, owing to the two coral red slashes under its throat.

The brown trout and his qualities are known to most anglers in this country, in which he is widely spread.

The grayling is a salmonid, having the adipose fin distinctive of that genus.

Next on our list of introduced fish comes salmo shasta *or the rainbow—whimsical fellow, merry fighter, leaper of leaps, provider of surprises, sheened like a Kang Shi porcelain vase.*

grassed it it weighed only two and a half pounds. It gave me the hardest fight I ever had from a trout. It was a thick, deep, perfectly shaped fish. Its condition factor must have been "tops." I guess it to have been a precocious fish that had run up out of season, for it had all the appearance of a fresh run fish. It surely was not an "old inhabitant," but it may of course have been one of last fall's run. Yet I have observed that the average of browns which I have caught in June and July are apt to be scrawny fish. When they start running up in mid-August they are fat and fit; they play well and "eat" well. It cannot be a question of "mending" for in June it is months since they spawned, and the authorities inform me that ten days suffices for these trout to recover from the act of spawning. I can only assume that the long winter period in some way affects them adversely.

There are, of course, some "old inhabitants" which are fine specimens, particularly in the Madison, where the shelter and the feed are both perfect for their growth and protection. These are fish which have over the years escaped all deadly offerings and continued to thrive in some "home" of their selection. I saw one of just over seven pounds caught on a fly in the Madison in August, on the 14th to be exact; it was a perfect fish in every respect. The next day I caught a similar but smaller brown of three pounds in about the same place, on a large salmon fly. I found, however, that these large resident fish do not play anything like so well as the running spawners. That is not "sour grapes," for nobody will deny the thrill of hooking an out-size fish, even if you can walk him in to the bank in record time. I once, back in Scotland, hooked and landed a salmon of nigh on forty-six pounds when fishing the Don with my good friend Gordon Lawson Johnston, so I know what a thrill it is; and that fish incidentally by no means came walking in.

Salmo shasta

Next on our list of introduced fish comes *salmo shasta* or the rainbow—whimsical fellow, merry fighter, leaper of leaps, provider of surprises, sheened like a Kang Shi porcelain vase. What the difference is between *shasta* and *irideus* I do not propose to discuss; it matters little; they are both our friend, the rainbow. When he takes to a seagoing life he becomes a steelhead. When he inhabits the McKenzie River, and some of the other rivers of Oregon, he becomes a redsides. His bar of pink then becomes no longer a sheen, but a more clearly defined bar of deep Ming red, as you might see it painted on a Wan Li vase. Yet they are all one and the same beloved rainbow to me.

He abounds in the waters of Yellowstone. He has his central depot in Hebgen Lake outside the Park and in Fish Lake within the Park. Out of Hebgen he is trapped at the stations referred to in my paragraph on the brown trout. In Fish Lake he is specialized in; there are none but rainbows there, and the streamlet up which they run to spawn is but a few feet wide.

You should go and see Fish Lake if only for its beauty and its evening peace and its surrounding carpet of flowers. It lies in a fold in the hills above Soda Butte, along the Cooke Mountain road. You may not angle in it. Even the road up to it is barred. So go and call on the Ranger at Soda Butte Station (it is right beside the road) and ask him to take you up one evening.

The lake was originally formed by the accident of a storm damming up a fold in the hills. Then came Mr. and Mrs. Beaver and completed the job in the efficient manner of their kind. Not only did they complete it, but ever since they have undertaken voluntarily the work of upkeep and repair. This year there was, alas, a local scarcity of aspen, which is the Beaver family's daily bread; so out across the hills they would trot of an evening to find their well-earned meals. Here was a chance for the ever-watching coyote. Mrs. Beaver and four out of the five little Beavers, instead of procuring their own dinner, became dinner for the preying coyotes. Now poor Mr. Beaver and his one remaining child grieve disconsolate. It seems to me to be high time that the coyotes were thinned out again. They are not picturesque, for in summer they never appear, or hardly ever, in the valleys where you and I roam. It is only when the snow begins to mantle the hills that they come down to the valleys in search of food, and then the tourists are all gone. Their toll on better and more beautiful wild life is too grievous to be overlooked.

Up above Fish Lake lies another little lake which

abounds in freshwater shrimp, the near-by existence of which adds greatly to the attractiveness of Fish Lake as a breeding centre; for these freshwater shrimp are an invaluable food for the parents of future generations of lusty rainbows.

If you look up to the hills behind you, from Fish Lake, you will notice the mouths of rocky caverns. It is to these caves that, when winter comes, many of the grizzly bears in the Park repair to hibernate and produce their young—queer little animals, these children of a 500-pound mother, bald as chihuahuas at birth and weighing but a mere nine ounces apiece. Explain me that one if you can.

I do not need to tell you much about the rainbow. You know him already for the most sporting of fish. He seems in the Yellowstone waters to be always in good condition, spring or fall. You will rarely catch a scrawny one. He rises to both wet and dry fly and generally runs about two pounds in weight, though I have caught them up to three pounds and a little over in the Madison and the Grayling. In Grebe Lake they run particularly big; there you get your four-pounders and better, but a catch of Yellowstone rainbows generally looks much like the Dionne family, peas out of a pod, as it were, and pretty as paint.

Salvelinus fontinalis

The last of our introduced river trout is *salvelinus fontinalis,* our speckled friend of the Eastern waters,

There remains, of the introduced fish, the lake trout or mackinaw.

PRIOR PAGE: *You should go and see Fish Lake if only for its beauty and its evening peace and its surrounding carpet of flowers.*

colloquially known as the Eastern brook. Let us call him the brook, for short. In colouration he is outstandingly beautiful; as a table fish he is second only to the Yellowstone cutthroat; and as sport yielder he stands high, for he is not an "easy" fish. When not definitely on the feed, he is hard to lure.

He is a fall spawner, like the brown. He is planted in various waters in the Park, particularly in the streams and lakes to the north. I do not know of any central depot from which ova are obtained by the trapping of tributaries. Curiously enough in six weeks of fishing and observation I have caught or come across very few *fontinalis,* though I have caught many hybrids in which the strain of *fontinalis* clearly showed.

The Rangers all have maps of the Park marked in coloured inks, showing in what waters various types of fish have been planted, each type being represented by a different colour. You should ask leave to study one of these maps; they are most informative.

Cristivomer namaycush

There remains, of the introduced fish, the lake trout or mackinaw. Let us refer to him under the latter and more distinctive title. He breeds in the lake, where he lies most of the time deep down. He grows to a large size, up in the sixties and seventies of pounds. In July of this year one of 22 pounds and one of 31 pounds were reported from Heart Lake. Save, however, in certain weather conditions, when he comes comparatively near to the surface, you have to go down and seek him out. For this you use a line of copper wire and other contraptions which are really outside the scope of this book. I have caught him up in Maine at the end of May on Grand Lake and Dobsis Lake, where I used to be a guest under the kindly roof of Byron Eldred. He is heavy and dogged to play, with no fireworks or surprises. I used to catch him on a live bait but the others used to troll for him with a beaded gear that looked much like a necklace out of King Tutankhamen's tomb. As a table fish he is famous, and he is dealt in commercially in large quantities. The commercial fish are, I presume, taken in nets.

So we have a noble variety and choice of fish for which to angle. Let us now go and see where and how we can best catch them.

CHAPTER FOUR

MOSTLY ABOUT LAKES

THE finest angling waters of the Yellowstone area are, in my humble opinion, the Yellowstone River on the one hand and on the other the group of rivers which connect with Hebgen Lake. These rivers are the Madison, South Fork, Grayling and Duck. Of these the Madison originates from the marriage of the Gibbon and the Firehole, and the Duck includes the Cougar, which is a small tributary of the Duck but eminently fishworthy. So in effect there are seven of these streams, but they run into the lake as four separate identities. I therefore propose to christen them the Four Rivers, and so refer to them throughout these pages. After the Yellowstone River and the Four Rivers, next in importance is the Gallatin River, important both for its length and for the quality of its fishing. Then come the Lamar, Bechler, Slough Creek, Pelican, Soda Butte and a variety of smaller streams.

You will no doubt have observed, if you have studied your map, that in that list there are considerable omissions—the Snake River, for instance, in the south of the Park, and the Gardiner River and various creeks in the north. I can only plead that in six weeks it was impossible to cover more ground. The Snake River is for the most part inaccessible except by pack-horse.

The rivers and creeks to the north, whilst being accessible, do not afford fishing which is comparable to those to which I have devoted my time. The latter in themselves comprise at a rough estimate more than a hundred miles of first-class fishing. I think that such a feat should satisfy the appetite of even the most ardent angler.

Before, however, we go stream fishing I must in duty bound make some reference to the lakes. Personally I would rather fish in a lake than not fish at all, but when streams are available lakes have to take a second place.

A glance at the map will show you that by far the biggest aquatic feature of the Park is Yellowstone Lake. It is the home of the cutthroats, as already described. It is accessible from its western edge, along which the road runs for some miles. It may be fished from the shore or from boats. If you stand of an evening at Fishing Bridge, you may see, perhaps, a hundred anglers casting every kind of lure into the lake, and mostly with success. They take fish up to one or one and a half pounds in weight. If you want to take larger ones you should hire a boat and fish around Stevenson Island, or in other likely spots which your boatman, who knows the water, will recommend. Your limit is five fish per day, so you may as well get good ones. Of course you may take your aunt and your mother-in-law along with you and, counting them as anglers, bring in fifteen fish! I have seen it done, but it can hardly be described as within the spirit of the law.

A glance at the map will show you that by far the biggest aquatic feature of the Park is Yellowstone Lake . . . It may be fished from the shore or from boats.

The latter of these is Jackson Lake. . . . There is an excellent camp on its shore, Wort's camp, where you may pass the night and wake up in the morning to look across the water at the snowy heights of the Grand Teton mountain range.

Flies are very successful as a lure, so you need not resort to spinners unless your preference is for them. In no event, however, must you use live bait in this or any other water in the Park. Unthinking anglers do not realize that when they bring in live bait they do not know what undesirable fish they may unintentionally liberate in the well-protected waters of the Park. The two outstanding dangers are suckers and carp, both of them spawn eaters and public enemies in trout waters. Never until five years ago was a sucker seen in Yellowstone Lake or any of its tributaries. To-day they are there, and they can only have been introduced by live bait anglers. I know of only one tributary which they infect as yet, but once established they are more than hard to eradicate. It seems to me that any infraction of the live bait rule should be punished by the exclusion of the guilty party from the Park for the whole season.

There are three other important lakes in the south of the Park and one which I might mention to the south of and outside the Park.

The latter of these is Jackson Lake. If you come up to Yellowstone from Denver and the south you will pass right by Jackson Lake. There is an excellent camp on its shore, Wort's camp, where you may pass the night and wake up in the morning to look across the water at the snowy heights of the Grand Teton mountain range. You may hire a motor boat and fish to your heart's content. Don't be deceived as to the size of the lake; the land facing you is not mainland but an island behind which stretch 22 miles of water, some of it excellent fishing ground. You see now why I said "motor boat" for, as you might expect, the best water is not the nearest.

As you enter Yellowstone Park from the south, you will pass the Snake River right at the entrance; then the Lewis River and falls. The Lewis River looks ideal for fishing but is not worth your attention. Then a little further on you will see Lewis Lake extending away to your left. The road runs along its shore for some little way. If you take a boat and cross it you will come on the far side to a channel which links it up with Shoshone Lake, a channel some three miles in length which affords excellent fly fishing. Both Lewis and Shoshone lakes afford excellent fishing. The best way to tackle them is to pack in from Thumb to Shoshone Lake and make your camp. There is every variety of trout to be had, including mackinaw, and these waters, being less accessible than most, are naturally less fished. I can imagine no more restful and sporting way to spend a week or so than to camp out on Shoshone. There are plenty of concerns who will make packing arrangements for you. Ask the Ranger at Thumb.

As you pass the camping grounds on the shore of Lewis Lake you will notice a track that runs off into the woods to your right. This is the trail into Heart Lake; you can drive down it only a short way; then you have to park your car and walk. The lake is some five miles distant. The five miles in would not be so

As you enter Yellowstone Park from the south, you will pass the Snake River right at the entrance. . . .

. . . then the Lewis River and falls.

bad, but the five miles out after a hard day's fishing, and with perhaps a 20-pound mackinaw on your back, are not so funny. So once more I recommend a pack in and a short stay.

There are in addition numberless small lakes all over these 3,400 square miles. The most important is Grebe Lake, to which I have referred as the home of the grayling. If you are in the Park in late August, when it is open to fishing, do not miss it. The fishing is definitely best either in the early morning or late evening. To reach it you turn off the Norris-Canyon road three miles on the Norris side of Canyon. When you have driven a couple of miles you will come to a locked barrier. Here you must park your car—and, by the way, never leave food in a parked car. The bears have can-opener paws and long-distance noses, and a car which has been "opened" by a bear is a depressing sight; I've seen one. From the barrier you hike in another two miles along the trail to the lake. Take long waders with you; short waders or rubber boots are not enough. When you reach the lake, work round to the right and fish the points where small creeks come in; also further round, by the marshes at the far side. Go warily in the marshes, or you will get a ducking, and a smelly ducking at that. There are plenty of four-pound rainbows, and when they take, they mean business; so see that your leader is in good shape and your knots well tied.

Due west of West Yellowstone lies Henry's Lake. It is actually in Idaho, in a little corner of Idaho which tucks itself up into the lap of Montana; so to fish here you must have an Idaho licence. You take road "191 South," which in point of fact runs west, out West Yellowstone to Ashton and Pocatello. You pass through the Targhee forest, over the divide; in about twenty miles you will see McGinn's Sun Valley Ranch. Here you turn right to Henry's Lake. Though not a big lake, it harbours big fish. It may be fished from the shore or from boats, which are available.

Then there is Hidden Lake, way up among the hills, but I do not want to take you too far afield. Hidden Lake has a great reputation for monsters. One evening this summer a fish of over 30 pounds was displayed on ice in a West Yellowstone tavern as having been caught there. The fish was in point of fact a salmon which had been sent up from the Pacific coast, so that anyone who knew his salmon was not taken in; but for one evening the inhabitants of the village, not being salmon wise, were a-buzz at the wonder from Hidden Lake. It was not a bad joke, for, of an evening, fish and fishing are the main topic in West Yellowstone. It certainly sold many glasses of beer that night, which I shrewdly suspect was a possibility well in the mind of the proprietor when he permitted the hoax to be carried out. But it was the reputation of Hidden Lake as a holder of monsters that made it possible!

As for the numberless small lakes in the Park, you must consult the Rangers, and if you have the Daniel Boone complex you may trek out and locate them one by one. I will not accompany you, if you will excuse

Due west of West Yellowstone lies Henry's Lake.

Some five or six miles along you will come to the edge of Hebgen Lake, which you have already descried in the distance.

me. Anno domini and the many wonderful stretches of flowing streams which await me are my ample excuse.

The most important lake of all I have left to the last, Hebgen Lake. It is an artificial reservoir made by the damming of the valley to the northwest of Yellowstone. It is the property of the Montana Power Company and its water is derived from the inflow of the Four Rivers. To save you from referring back, I will repeat that they are the Madison, South Fork, Grayling and Duck (the latter including its tributary, the Cougar). They all four flow into Hebgen at its southeastern end, and there three of them die; for at the outlet of the lake flows one river, and one only, the Madison, gathering strength as it goes, until finally, with the Gallatin and the Jefferson, it in turn loses its identity and merges into the Missouri River.

If you leave West Yellowstone by "191 North," toward Bozeman, you will come some ten miles out to a fork. Here you take number "1" to the left, the Ennis-Butte road. Some five or six miles along you will come to the edge of Hebgen Lake, which you have already descried in the distance. Hebgen is the key to the excellence of the angling district of Yellowstone. Had the Montana Power Company not had occasion to create this lake, Yellowstone would have been a good fishing district but not the superlative one which it has been, and which I hope it will remain for years to come—not one about which to write a book, even a poor book like the present one.

The reason for the importance of Hebgen lies in two facts. It is a wonderfully propitious water for the growth of trout. The food supply is excellent and probably there are other intangibles which make trout

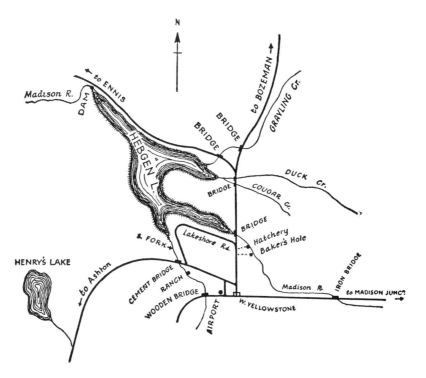

happy in it. Therefore you have a great stock of lusty fish. Then you have the other great factor—the fact that no less than four rivers lie up-stream of it, into which the fish can run to spawn, and not just four rivers but four of the most beautiful trout angling streams in the whole continent of America. Up these streams pour the fat fish of Hebgen—browns and brooks in the fall, rainbows, grayling and cutthroats in the spring—driven onward by the procreative urge. The earlier they run, the higher they go; for in that manner nature provides an even distribution of fish along the streams. And, as they go, they are yours for the skilful casting of a fly. Please use a fly, and please don't kill them in numbers in Hebgen. The rivers are so much more sporting a battle-ground.

So there, you see, you have an angler's Utopia in itself. When you add the Park with its lakes and other rivers—Yellowstone, Lamar, Slough, Bechler, Snake, Gardiner and many a lesser creek—and when you add 50 miles or more of the Gallatin, I think you must admit that you have a fishing centre worthy of your skill and attention. But the nucleus, the very red of this heart, is Hebgen and the Four Rivers. I emphasize this with a double purpose, because I want you to appreciate it should you be going to visit Yellowstone, and also because at the end of this book I am going to point out what I believe to be great dangers to this Eden and to make some suggestions for warding off those dangers; and in those dangers Hebgen is intimately concerned.

You will take careful notice of the shape of Hebgen. Disregarding detailed irregularities, it splits, in its main form, at the southern end into two wings, a northern and a southern wing, divided by elevated and timbered country which at the splitting point—or Narrows as it is called—curls round into a knob or butte shaped like a piece of a jig-saw puzzle. The southern wing in turn has a sub-wing on its southern side. Into

the southern wings run the Madison and the South
Fork, the Madison into the main southern wing and
the South Fork into the sub-wing. Into the northern
wing run the Duck to the south and the Grayling to
the north.

I want you to be clear about this, because in the
summer these two wings are frequently dry, and the
rivers flow on in their old beds and become most
profitably fishable for several miles, as they run through
the flats which, when the water is high, are completely
submerged. Did I not explain this with care you might
wonder later when I talk about fishing in stretches of
rivers which to all appearances do not exist as such. In
the summer of 1937 I fished the Grayling on foot right
up to the butte at the Narrows.

The Montana Power Company is an industrial concern, as its title indicates. Its function is to supply
electric power, and the preservation of fish life must,
of necessity, be a secondary consideration to it. In the
last two years the calls for power have been exceptionally heavy. The Fort Peck project, in particular,
has put heavy calls upon it. The result has been that
Hebgen has had to be let down to disastrously low
levels. I am given to understand that the Fort Peck
project is now near completion and also that the Power
Company is constructing further power units at Flat-
head Lake. It is hoped, according to recent press ar-
ticles, that these two facts combined will enable the
Company to build up the water volume of Hebgen
again from the spring of 1938 onward.

Practically all of our listed trout are to be found in Hebgen, except the mackinaw; but by far the most numerous are the rainbows and the browns. The lake is fishable either from the shore or from boats, and an immense number of fish (for there is a liberal limit of 10 per day) are taken out by rod and line from this capital stock every season—far, far too many, in my humble opinion, but of that later. Boats may be hired either at the Narrows or up near the dam. Fishing is of course best in the mornings and evenings. Fly is the best lure and taken eagerly when the fish are feeding.

At the end of this book I express certain views about the curtailment of fishing in Hebgen when the water is low, because at these times it becomes massacre rather than sport; but when the water is reasonably high Hebgen affords excellent and legitimate angling. Why, however, one should seek out these fish in the lake when one can have much better sport with them as they come up the rivers, I personally fail to understand. However, it is proverbially impossible to argue about tastes, so we will leave it at that.

CHAPTER FIVE

ABOUT THE FOUR RIVERS

NOW, after these preliminaries, let us go fishing, stream fishing, which is the only fishing for me. I recall a friend of Leander McCormick's in the old days on the Test, whose name at this distance of time escapes me, who whenever the supreme moment came for departure to the waterside was invariably heard to mutter to himself, "This is all very exciting." Very reverently, very sincerely he would mutter it, like grace before meals. It seemed, and still seems, to me to sum up in a very simple phrase the eternal truth about angling. Who doesn't know that tremor of expectation which fills all anglers' breasts with butterflies as they move off to their day's adventures, to the happenings that lie in store—odd happenings, happenings both glad and sad, sometimes incredible happenings? *"Credo quia incredibile"* cries the angler in his heart. Though friends deride, he knows, knows that in the course of any day's angling the impossible is always possible, always capable of defeating all the laws of chance and of making an honest man of Ananias.

The Madison

The most important of the Four Rivers is the Madison. It comes into being at the confluence of the Gib-

The most important of the Four Rivers is the Madison. It comes into being at the confluence of the Gibbon and the Firehole, right where the National Park idea was born.

If some evening you feel a desire for amusement rather than hard fishing, take your lightest rod and tackle and cast a line on the Gibbon in Virginia Meadows . . .

bon and the Firehole, right there where the National Park idea was born. It will therefore be logical to describe first its parent rivers, even as in any biography credit is first given to the parents who gave life to the great man whose history is to be unfolded.

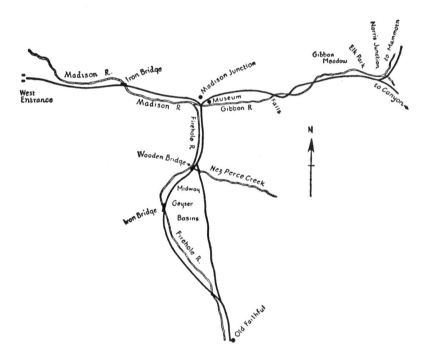

The Gibbon River first appears to view, for practical purposes, in Virginia Meadows, between Canyon and Norris Junctions. You will not be interested to track it to its source and beyond its fishable points. Even in Virginia Meadows it is as yet but a small stream, so small that you may jump across it, if you be young and agile. Yet you must not laugh at it as

you jump, for somehow it already has the serious dignity of a river with a purpose. Already it harbours good
trout under its grassy banks, hybrids, many of them,
but lusty and quick and fully worthy of your skill. At
Norris Junction a tributary comes in from the north
and joins the Gibbon, running now busy and fresh
from its fall over the Virginia Cascades. If some evening you feel a desire for amusement rather than hard
fishing, take your lightest rod and tackle and cast a
line on the Gibbon in Virginia Meadows and Norris
Meadows. It may be a new experience, angling in such
narrow waters, an experience both amusing and fruit-
ful.

At Norris the newly merged concern makes a detour around the acrid geyser basin with its columns of
steam and sulphuric odours. I for one don't blame it;
but it takes no apparent taint from its proximity to
this devil's laboratory. It returns to us on the high road
at Elk Park, now grown to adolescence, and as it meanders, curve after curve, through the lovely and
peaceful meadow, it seems to say, "Now I am ready
for you anglers; come and do your worst."

If you take up the challenge, as you surely must,
you will need all your skill; for all is open and above-
board in this contest. There are no bushes or high
grasses for your concealment, no subterfuges possible.
It is you *versus* the open river. As you fish it, you will
be facing all the quarters of the globe in turn, as it
ribbons its way back and forth; so if there be a breeze,
keep a thought to this fact or you will have some sorry

*At Norris the newly merged concern makes a detour around the acrid geyser
basin with its columns of steam and sulphuric odours.*

*From Elk Park the Gibbon commences to fall in disarray over the Chocolate
Pots, as they are called, for it has many a foot to fall before it meets its mate,
the Firehole . . .*

tangles to untie. If perchance you catch no fish, do not say, "They are not there." I have seen them, and when luck has been my way I have caught them, but they are not easy. Your foot must fall lightly on the grass, that it be not a tocsin of alarm, and your fly must fall like down upon the water, for this is kittle fishing, no work for a novice or a bungler. And please, oh please, do not desecrate this gentle stream with spinner, worm or other frightfulness. Had I my way you would be outlaw by the very act. When you have seen the Gibbon in the meadows you will agree with me; and if you agree with me I wish you joy of your evening, a perfect evening with some good rises, some well taken, others missed—for therein of a truth lies the salt of a day's angling—I wish you, say, a couple of brace of nice fish to take home-along, and the big one left behind with your favourite fly in his cheek; not out of meanness, this last, but in order to tempt you back another day. But if you do not agree with me, if you resort to spinners and other foul measures, then I can only wish for the early demise of your rabbit or pet canary, an ancient formula of disapproval and one which would seem, I admit, grossly unfair to the bunny and the bird.

From Elk Park the Gibbon commences to fall in disarray over the Chocolate Pots, as they are called, for it has many a foot to fall before it meets its mate, the Firehole—so many feet in fact that it decides not to take them all in one stride. So half a mile or so after the Chocolate Pots it "picks itself up, dusts itself off" and slides into Gibbon Meadow where it challenges the angler "all over again."

Gibbon Meadow is Elk Park in a slightly larger size. The meadow is larger, the river slightly broader. Whether the trout are bigger is up to you to find out. Toward evening the elk and their young come slowly out of the distant forest, browsing as they make their way slowly toward the water. In the distance, steam from a hidden geyser rises from among the fir trees, as though some giant were cooking his evening meal. The female elks emit occasional bellows, queer mixture of lion's roar and ass's bray, startling when heard for the first time, particularly if, as happened to me, the elk be near at hand yet unseen.

You will find it hard to tear yourself away from Gibbon Meadow until darkness overtakes you, so make no promises to wife or friend of a punctual return on that evening.

After Gibbon Meadow the river has to make up for its delay and starts tumbling again, this time in very earnest, until finally down it goes over the falls with a crash. Between Gibbon Meadow and the foot of the falls I do not recommend you to give it any of your time, but between the falls and its final arrival at Madison Junction there are some five or six miles of the prettiest wet fly water you could wish to see; and don't forget, the Hebgen trout come up this far, so mark off a couple of days on your calendar for this section of the Gibbon. The last mile, where it runs into the meadows at the junction, is beautiful, but it is ter-

After Gibbon Meadow the river has to make up for its delay and starts tumbling again, this time in very earnest . . .

PRIOR PAGE: *Toward evening the elk and their young come slowly out of the distant forest, browsing as they make their way slowly toward the water. In the distance, steam from a hidden geyser rises from among the fir trees, as though some giant were cooking his evening meal.*

. . . between the falls and its final arrival at Madison Junction there are some five or six miles of the prettiest wet fly water you could wish to see. . . .

The last mile, where it runs into the meadows at the junction, is beautiful . . .

ribly overfished, lying as it does at the junction of two main roads. For that reason I regretfully let this piece of water alone. Did I decide to fish it I would do so at crack o' dawn.

Now what of the Firehole, co-parent of the Madison? Perhaps the first thing to note about it is a local peculiarity which is new in my experience. It absorbs the overflow of numberless geysers, and yet the trout appear to be totally unaffected by this phenomenon. Neither the resultant warmth of the water nor the addition of a strong chemical content seems to bother them a whit. It is claimed by some that the warmth of the river induces worms in the trout, but I do not believe that there is any foundation for this belief in fact. Like so many popular fallacies it has gained a parrotlike and unthinking credence. You will occasionally discover worms in trout from most of these waters, lying like partially straightened hair-springs when you split your fish for eating. They are entirely harmless to the human being, so on the rare occasion when you may come across one do not let it "put you off." The life of this worm is a cycle in which birds play as important a part as the trout. It is only the larval form which occurs in the trout, and I find it hard to believe that both birds and fish conspire together to make the Firehole their favourite river for the combination required for the propagation of the worm.

The Firehole harbours very large trout. It is highly improbable that many running fish get over the falls and cascades which occur quite low down, near Madison Junction. The planted fish and local inhabitants undoubtedly prosper greatly. There is a fine food supply in the river, and that by my judgment outweighs almost any disadvantage save absolute pollution. But let us take it more in detail.

You need not pay attention to the Firehole above Old Faithful, but from this point down it will pay you to study every yard of it. For some four or five miles after Old Faithful, it runs just out of sight of the road, peeping through at times to assure us that it is still there. These few miles are excellent looking water but I never found time to fish them.

Then suddenly the river swings away to avoid the Midway geyser basin around which it makes a big curve. To me a single geyser or hot pool or similar phenomenon may be interesting and capable of great beauty. A general geyser basin, however, such as Midway or Norris, seems a blot upon the landscape. It reminds me of the Somme as it appeared in 1918.

The river does not return to the road until some five miles further down, five miles, that is, of road but many more of river run. It returns under a wooden plank bridge just below where the Nez Perce runs in and joins forces with the Firehole. From a point above Midway an old road runs off and, like the river, makes a detour around the basin, returning over the wooden bridge just referred to, so that by virtue of this old road you have easy access to these miles of excellent water. Some of the best fishing on the Firehole is to be found between the wooden bridge and Midway. I

Now what of the Firehole, co-parent of the Madison?

It [the Firehole] absorbs the overflow of numberless geysers . . .

It is highly improbable that many running fish get over the falls and cascades which occur quite low down, near Madison Junction.

A general geyser basin, however, such as Midway or Norris, seems a blot upon the landscape. It reminds me of the Somme as it appeared in 1918.

met one angler who had such good fortune there that he confined the whole of his holiday to this section of water. If you are coming up from Madison Junction and cross the wooden bridge, you will find an excellent "run" about a quarter of a mile up-stream. In August I have watched the trout at this point leaping out of the water after large red dragon-flies which they were taking in full flight.

A mile or so further on you will come to an iron bridge, with a hot geyser pool on the right. Do not park your car down-wind of the sulphur fumes; I once did with unfortunate results. Both up-stream and down-stream of the bridge is excellent fishing. Just up-stream of it there is a fast run of water about four feet deep which is as pretty a lie for a big fish as you will find in a day's march. It is all good; now that you are there you have only to walk up and down the banks and choose your spot. If you want a good dry fly stretch, take the track which leads across the open in a north-easterly direction from the hot pool by the iron bridge. In about half a mile it will bring you to a belt of trees and a full stop. On the other side of the belt of trees lies a stretch of beautiful gliding water worthy of the Hampshire Test. If you are a dry fly man you will probably spend many evenings here.

But I will not tire you with repeated indications of my favourite spots. The fun is in locating your own; but remember, over the wooden bridge is your route to the good places.

Nez Perce Creek I have never fished, but it is highly

spoken of and I believe that, though small, it holds good trout. Another day I would much like to try it. I mention it to avoid any implication that by silence I am condemning it.

From the wooden bridge down-stream to Madison Junction, the Firehole runs beside the main road all the way, so that it is visible and accessible by a competent angler. For some three miles it runs much like the Madison in the meadows, wide, clear, well weeded, smooth of surface, very very tempting. It is an excellent stretch of water with fine fish in it, but fish which need some catching. I have heard anglers claim that this is the best stretch of water in the Park. *Quot homines tot sententiæ*—there are so many "bests" among Yellowstone waters. Anyway this is a stretch which you cannot pass up.

After these three miles of smooth water the river breaks, first into a trot and then into a gallop as it makes its way to the cascades and the falls. Prior to the big tumble, there are some beautiful fast wet fly pools, with the best lies on the far side. Wade carefully here, for the bottom is rocky and uneven, and the current strong. There are some fine pools too below the falls, still more dangerous of access but worth while if you be young and agile.

And so to Madison Junction where we left the Gibbon waiting for us. Here under the lee of the mountain in the green meadows the two rivers converge and fuse, and out of this fusion is born the Madison, first and foremost of the Four Rivers.

Then suddenly the river swings away to avoid the Midway geyser basin around which it makes a big curve.

*If you are coming up from Madison Junction and cross the wooden bridge,
you will find an excellent "run" about a quarter of a mile upstream.*

A mile or so further on you will come to an iron bridge, with a hot geyser pool on the right. . . . Just up-stream of it there is a fast run of water about four feet deep which is as pretty a lie for big fish as you will find in a day's march.

*Nez Perce Creek I have never fished, but it is highly spoken of and I believe that,
though small, it holds good trout. Another day I would much like to try it.*

From the wooden bridge down-stream to Madison Junction, the Firehole runs beside the main road all the way, so that it is visible and accessible by a competent angler.

FACING PAGE: *Prior to the big tumble, there are some beautiful fast wet fly pools, with the best lies on the far side*

The distance from Madison Junction to the West Gate of the Park at West Yellowstone is some fourteen miles. For about ten of these fourteen miles the road and river run side by side. It is natural both from the structural and the scenic standpoints that the Park roads should have been built paralleling the rivers. It is also very convenient for anglers. The Lewis, Yellowstone, Gibbon, Firehole, Madison, Lamar, Soda Butte and Gallatin—all of them, either for the whole or a considerable part of their existence, add joy to your progress by running along beside you. I know of few, if any, districts where angling streams thus parallel the roads for mile after mile. The Rhine, the Danube, the Thames, yes; but they are great rivers carrying the burden of commerce and transport upon their broad backs. Bridges are generally the only points of vantage for anglers to examine the state and quality of fishing streams as they pass. Years ago, when I used to fish in Austria and Bavaria with Trinks, we were driven by a stolid German chauffeur named Franz. At every bridge to which we came Trinks would shout "Halt, Franz!" and we would get out and peer into the depths for a while, held there by the irresistible fascination of the flowing water and the fish hanging in the stream. Then on we would go again until the next bridge came into view. To Franz it was all a mystery what we did, just gazing into the waters; but, having the military upbringing of all Germans, he soon acquired the routine and would stop on any and every bridge, regardless of the word of command. He got

so that he would have stopped on London Bridge or
the Pont Henri IV or the Golden Gate and would have
been bitterly disappointed if we did not get out and
peer into the dark waters.

These ten miles are all of them first-class fishing
water. A glance at them will tell you that, without
any confirmation from me. There is not an ell of them
that you can afford to miss, if you are an enthusiast and
a thorough fisherman; and to be thorough is the beginning of success in all angling. One of the first lessons
which I learned from my old friend and mentor John
Sharpe of Aberdeen was to be thorough, to "cover my
water."

The water of the Madison is warmer than that of
the other three rivers in the group, a characteristic
which, of course, it inherits from the Firehole. It is
extremely clear and throughout the stretch of which
we are speaking is amply provided with aquatic plant
life, which provides both food and shelter for the fish.
It varies in width, I would say at a guess, from sixty to
a hundred feet. Its bed is extremely varied. At times
it is composed of lava and volcanic matter. There is
a stretch of this nature about two miles below the
junction. Here big fish lie under cover of the lava
ledges. Your feet, as you wade, may seem to be on
bottom, but in fact below you are unseen caverns where
big fish hide. At other points the bed is composed of
small rocks and large stones which, where they exist,
add speed and action to the river. For long stretches,
however, in the section under discussion, the bed is

At times it is composed of lava and volcanic matter. There is a stretch of this nature about two miles below the junction. Here big fish lie under cover of the lava ledges.

There is at this point a big bend in the river where for a mile or so it leaves the immediate proximity of the road, though not its view.

soft, composed of what is apparently a form of sandy gravel. In these stretches the bed is curiously uneven, dropping into deep depressions and rising into high mounds, so that you may never wade with ease, and certainly never in anything but high waders. Even in them you will have to tack your way to and fro in order to come safely in and out. There can be no going straight ahead, for that would soon end in a plunge into one of the depressions.

The consequence of this unevenness of bed is a constant swirl on the surface of the water, a never-ending series of miniature whirlpools. Which came first, the uneven bottom or the whirlpools, I do not know; it is the old story of the owl and the egg. Occasionally they form rings which aggravatingly simulate a rising fish. I have often been thrown into a palpitation by them. The worst of them, however, is that they play the very devil with your line and fly. The latter is always in danger of taking on a drag and the former of drowning. There is one place in particular, about three miles below the junction, where this phenomenon is at its worst, and in that very sector lie some particularly good fish. There is at this point a big bend in the river where for a mile or so it leaves the immediate proximity of the road, though not its view. A large meadow intervenes, round which the river runs under the lee of the far hillside. I have spent hours at this point trying to get a dry fly presented aright to the big fish as they rise to the evening cloud of millers. For one or two casts my line would float and then, down, down, it would go. And even when my line did float, the intervening eddies would turn my fly into a ballet dancer, until finally it too would expire like Pavlova in "The Swan."

I discussed this experience with several competent anglers. The only consolation which I got was to know that I was not alone in it. One, in particular, who has fished the Madison for years, told me that he has long since given up the attempt to fish a dry fly among the eddies, where the bed is uneven. I have since wondered whether the chemical content of the water coming down from the geysers *via* the Firehole may have some effect upon one's line. I am no chemist, but it seems to me to be a possible explanation of the impossibility of preventing the line from drowning.

I did indeed have one success in this meadow which I will record, not for my own glorification but in order that, if you feel so disposed, you may go and do likewise. It was, by my diary, June 28th. I had spent an exasperating hour on the near bank watching my line and fly drown whilst the fish rose all unconcerned around me. Suddenly I noticed, right under the tall grasses on the far bank, in the very elbow of the bend, the kidney-shaped whorl of a big fish sucking in flies. Anyone who has fished a Hampshire chalk stream cannot mistake that sign. "There," said I to myself, *more diplomatico*, "is the way round," for is there not always a way round? No more waterlogging; just a nice brown and white bi-visible, dropped gently onto those grasses and then lightly shaken off onto the water, should do the trick. But before trying my "way round" I had first to find a way across, without myself getting waterlogged; for where I stood the holes were too deep. Down-stream I sped for half a mile, my heart beating with the excitement of my new strategy. Finally I made the crossing, though only by inches, and proceeded to put my plan into execution. Gentlemen, it worked!

In one and a half hours of mosquito-ridden heaven, I netted six big fish and was twice broken. The two which I kept were just under three pounds each, and none at a fair estimate was a whit under two and a half pounds. One of my captives gave me a special ride. He ran down-stream under a fallen tree which was lying sunken across the river bed. I played him for some few minutes with my rod lying flat under water, and most of my person immersed; but I worked him safely back, and no wetting could have damped my enthusiasm when I returned to camp and supper that night. It was not until my return in August that I attempted a repetition of the great event. Alas, as so often happens with repetitions, it fell flat. The only parties to the old act who remained were myself and the mosquitoes, the latter in better form than ever. The trout would not play any more. There are moments in life which one can never recapture; perhaps it is as well. That evening with the "bankers" on the far side of the meadows at the big bend on the Madison will always remain for me one of my great and memorable angling occasions.

From the meadows on down to the iron bridge is

all fine fishing, particularly for the observant angler whose sixth sense will warn him of the presence of big fish. There are certain famous spots of which I will speak in this book, because they are much spoken of by others and failure to pay them some small homage might be attributed to ignorance. My object, however, is to conduct you to the river as intelligently and directly as I can, and then, having thrown what light I usefully may upon the general characteristics of the water, to leave you there to work out your own happiness and find your own fish, for the fun is in the finding.

Among the famous "holes" is one which you will come upon a little further down-stream from the meadows. It is called the Nine Mile Hole, so named because it lies about nine miles east of the west entrance to the Park. Therefore by simple calculation it should be something over four miles from Madison Junction coming in the other direction. You will recognize it by the little promontory of grass with a big round rock standing by itself at the water's edge. There is a steep little run down onto the promontory from the road and another one back onto the road.

It is the most overfished of any hole that I know, this Nine Mile Hole. Time and again I have run those nine miles, only to find it occupied. I have stopped on my way home of an evening and found anglers settling in on the promontory for the night, so as to be first on the scene at dawn. Yet, despite all the attention it receives, it is still a good bet for a brace of heavy fish. You must try it. On the far side you will observe

two patches of floating weed. Start fishing about a
hundred paces above the upper patch of weed and fish
slowly down, taking care to cast your fly well over to
the far side of the hole. You will of course need high
waders. Unless you see a fish moving near the surface,
which I doubt, use a heavy fly; or, if your fly be light,
pinch on a split shot to the leader just above the fly.
You will do best if you go down to these fish instead
of asking them to come up to you.

On one occasion, when I was waiting my turn, the
"outgoing tenant" came over and spoke to me. It
seemed he was a local angler. He claimed that some
years back he was "one of the discoverers of the hole,"
whatever that meant. He went on to inform me with
ill-concealed pride that not so many years ago he had,
in one morning, killed in the Nine Mile Hole 15 trout
weighing over 74 pounds. "But," said he, with an in-
jured air, "those days are gone forever."

"No wonder," I replied, with equally ill-concealed
irony; but I fear my meaning was lost upon him.

I got one good laugh out of this hole. Staying in my
camp in West Yellowstone was a delightful old angler
who much favoured the hole and who loved to get an
hour to himself on it. Morning after morning he would
rise betimes and, "after being connubially kissed," he
would start out to be the first through the Park gates,
which open to vehicular traffic at six o'clock. Yet upon
arrival there he would invariably find, up to his waist
in the good Madison, a well known local fish-hog,
standing like some evil heron in command of the

water. Time and again the incident would recur until I suggested to my old friend the explanation, which was simple, for all that the fish-hog had to do was to park his car inside the gates over night, walk in at 5.50 A. M. and get a ten-minute head start. The remedy, I suggested, was equally obvious, a well and truly incised puncture by the dark of the moon, but whether my friend ever resorted to it I did not care to ask. There might be such a thing as being an accessory before the act!

The water both above and below the iron bridge is peculiarly lovely and quite, quite in the first class. There are some very deep runs, one in particular on the near side of the great rocks which stand like sentinels along the far bank under the forest edge below the bridge. I have seen splendid fish caught here on both dry and wet fly. It was here that on one occasion I watched and learned what was to me a new technique, dry fly fishing down-stream. By casting a long line with a last-minute backward pull, so that a coil of slack line lay between him and his fly, the angler succeeded in netting several nice fish. As the spare line paid out, the fly came over the rising fish just at the right moment and before drag set in. It needed accurate adjustment. What would have happened had another fish a yard above the intended victim taken the fly, I do not know, but I can guess; a swift ejection and a good-bye before the angler could strike. However, I subsequently tried it myself and caught a two-pound brown on a dry Parmacheene Belle. No one was more surprised than my-

You will recognize it by the little promontory of grass with a big round rock standing by itself at the water's edge.

There are some very deep runs, one in particular on the near side of the great rocks which stand like sentinels along the far bank under the forest edge below the bridge.

self and a tourist from British Columbia who was watching the experiment. He and his wife and ginger-headed son enjoyed the fish and my good luck. It is all right as an amusing specialty, this down-stream dry fly fishing, but I cannot recommend it as a standard technique.

Most evenings by the sentinel rocks below the iron bridge the elk come down out of the forest and drink and lie around. They evidently feel safe with the steep fir-clad slope behind them and the river in front. I have often tried to take a picture of them, but the river is too wide to give it any value. I did once have a close-up of them, but without benefit of camera. It was in this wise. I was homeward bound and just approaching the iron bridge when a brown bear made a clumsy dash for first honours. I slowed down and let him have the road. Then, when we were on the bridge, his nonchalance annoyed me, so I horned at him and got him hustling. His rear view, as, with loss of all his former dignity, he shuffled along, was a comedy of movement. It and the dirty look which he gave me as he turned off the bridge sent me into fits of laughter. I turned to jeer at him as he disappeared, and when I looked forward again into the setting sun there were my friends, the elk, right under the nose of my car. Just for this once they had crossed the river to browse and take the evening air. I all but had elk steak for supper that evening.

Let me warn you about that westward drive home if you camp in West Yellowstone, for you will make it many an evening. The setting sun is blinding until it gets down behind the mountain tops. That in itself is bad, and, since the road winds in and out in a succession of curves, you will all the time be running from light into shade and from shade into blinding light. I think of the two the former is the greater danger, but either is apt to render you for a moment completely helpless. There is only one thing to do. Stop until you get your bearings again, or you may add one more to the many accidents which arise from this cause.

If you are returning westward through the Park of an evening, I would recommend you in any event, and regardless of the point of safety to which I have just referred, to wait until the sun drops down behind the mountain tops. I am thinking of your sense of the beautiful. This great playground in which you are passing golden hours is ringed around with mountains. It is too vast for you to see them all; yet, fish you where you will, when you raise your eyes there they will be, mountains of all shapes and many hues. In the sunlight they are proud and distant, but, as you approach the western gate in the red glory of the sunset, they will take outline all around you, as far as the eye can reach; they will come closer to you than by daylight—mysterious, unreal, in the crimson of the dying day, like some great stage setting to the play of life. I never tired of this homeward drive and the glory of the mountains framed by the setting sun.

Some three or four miles before you get to the west

The great playground in which you are passing golden hours is ringed around with mountains. It is too vast for you to see them all; yet, fish you where you will, when you raise your eyes there they will be, mountains of all shapes and many hues. In the sunlight they are proud and distant, but, as you approach the western gate in the red glory of the sunset, they will take outline all around you, as far as the eye can reach; they will come closer to you than by daylight—mysterious, unreal, in the crimson of the dying day, like some great stage setting to the play of life.

. . . the elk come down out of the forest and drink and lie around.

entrance, the river leaves the road-side. For the last mile or so it has become less interesting, just to ease our regrets. So now we must go and look for it and find out where it goes, watching the plan as we go. For we are now coming to some ten miles of the best trout fishing ever, ten miles with hardly a yard in it that is not good. My plan only claims to be a rough plan; it makes no claim to accuracy of scale; it completely disregards bends in the roads, but it serves to show you where the Madison River goes to and how you may best get to it. If it succeeds in that, it is all I ask of it.

You will observe that what it does in principle is to cut across the angle formed by the Park road and the Bozeman road, where it appears again under the bridge on its way out to Hebgen Lake. It passes out of the authority of the Park only a mile or two before it hits the Bozeman road, a mile or two riverwise, I mean. This is my favourite section of the Madison, because of its greater solitude and wildness and also because of the swifter movement of its waters.

But let us get to it. One mile before you come to the western gate of the Park (or one mile in, if you start from West Yellowstone) you will see a dirt road turning off to the north side of the road. It is the only one; it may be identified by the STOP plaque which warns outcoming traffic to stop before coming into the main road. You turn in at this road. In about six hundred yards it splits right, left, and straight on. You keep straight on, passing under the telephone wire and down

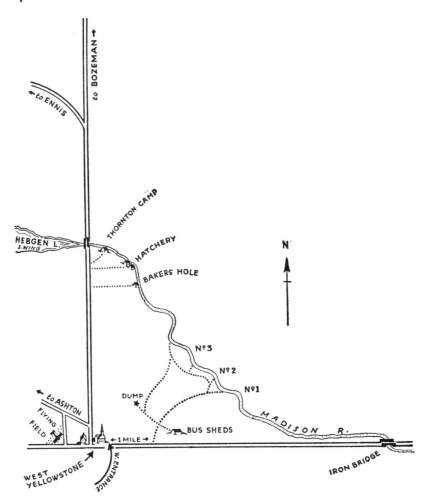

a sharp little incline. At the foot of this slope there is again a choice of right, left, or straight on. The right-hand road leads to the garage of the Park omnibuses, locally known as the Barns. Straight on takes you to the river, so again you go straight on. You may, however, make a mental note that the left-hand road at this point leads you direct to points further down-stream. Another day you may want to take this route to save time.

Having continued straight on, you will in quite a short distance come to the bluff above the river. As you reach the river the track spurs off to the right to where an overhead cable crosses the stream. At this point you park your car, for you are now at what is colloquially known as Hole No. 1.

You are now faced by a river quite different in character from the one you left alongside the road in the Park. All seems changed. The bed of the river is now composed of large stones, dark in colour; the aquatic weeds and plants have disappeared; the calm surface of the waters has changed into dancing wavelets which chant a merry tune as they go. "Perfect wet fly water," you mutter to yourself, and you are right. It *is* perfect wet fly water, with any number of good fish in it, and it remains perfect wet fly water all the way from now until it disappears into Hebgen Lake beyond the Bozeman road. Please don't read me to mean that dry fly cannot be used. I have often changed over successfully to catch a given fish that showed itself; but as a whole the fish do not "show" in this water which truthfully bespeaks a wet fly.

Hole No. 1 lies both up-stream and down-stream of the cable, but you should start fishing the straight water from half a mile further up. It is one of three holes, all of which are famous in local story and all indicated on my rough sketch. They are indeed good holding pools, which never seem to tire of yielding up fish. No. 1 to me has been the least kind and No. 2 the most kind. No. 3 holds, I fancy, most fish of all; but No. 2 is my preference of the three, with no explanation offered. *De gustibus,* you know. Incidentally, No. 2 serves a second purpose for me. On Sunday mornings I run my car down into the shallow edge of the pool and give it its weekly bath. The road runs down the bluff at this pool and permits of direct approach to the water, and the bed of the pool is hard, so that you need have no fear of getting stuck. So there I stand in my rubber boots, whistling like an hostler and rubbing my good steed down with water running fresh all the time. In West Yellowstone every drop of water has to be pumped, and cars just go dirty, and if there is one thing which I dislike it is the appearance of a dirty car.

Surprisingly enough, it does not disturb either fish or fishermen, this washing process. One Sunday morning, when I was swishing away, I saw a fish move in mid-stream just out from the round rock which you will notice by the near shore, toward the latter end of the pool. As each morning angler came by, I advised him of the fact, but not one of them touched my fish— or any other fish for that matter, for it was an unpropitious morning and the fish were being difficult. No less than seven anglers passed by, one after the other, for it is like that in the Park on Sunday mornings.

Then came an eighth, a portly fellow of merry aspect, his hat a-dangle with ironmongery. Once again

I did my civil best to aid another's sport. He thanked me and replied, "Say, if he's there, this airplane spinner will get him." On he went, the air droning with the hum of his terrible contraption as he cast it with amazing skill from a patient and uncomplaining fly rod. Fifteen minutes later he returned.

"Well, your fish wasn't there," he said, more in sorrow than in anger.

"Oh, but it is there," I replied. "I saw it."

"Then why not catch it?" was his mischievous comeback.

Well, if he couldn't rise the fish, he succeeded in rising me. Then and there I dropped my Sunday morning chore, fitted up a dry fly rod, put on my favourite brown and white bi-visible, and down after him I went. Out of the corner of my eye I saw a smile on the face of my portly and good-humoured friend. I read his thoughts, but, the Heavens be praised, he was wrong. At the second offering the fish took it with a bang, a nice rainbow a shade over two pounds.

"Well, I'm blowed," said my friend. "I've often heard about this dry fly business, but I reckoned it was all hooey. Say, can you put me wise how to get an outfit? I'm sold on it." Of such trivial incidents are converts born.

The laugh of the story is really on me, for I never did finish my Sunday morning chore. Once a mounted rod is in my hand, I am lost to all other duties. I have wondered since whether he thought of that!

Please do not by this talk of pools be deceived into

thinking that they are the only places to fish. Far from it. I have caught just as good and just as many fish in the ordinary run of the river. Whilst pools are good congregating places, they are also good hiding places and good sulking places. Were I fishing for a prize of the fullest creel of the day, I would select the ordinary run of the stream, knowing that in two to three feet of water my fly is more likely to be seen and the fish more likely to be on the move. There are in this section of the Madison an amazing number of good fish lies; in fact it is a sequence of them for mile upon mile; and the more you fish it, the more you find.

Once again, wear high waders; don't listen to the rubber boot adviser. He is all wet, and so will his boots be if he tries to get to the good reaches.

Another warning: Beware beaver holes. This advice refers not only to this stretch of the Madison but to the Grayling, Duck and Bechler and to all rivers where you notice the piled-up stick houses which are evidence of the existence of beavers. It is quite serious advice. This admirably industrious and otherwise benevolent animal has one serious defect. He builds himself this vast structure composed of intertwined sticks (I am told that he builds it "solid" and then carves out the inner rooms with his teeth), into which he enters, not from the top or the sides, as you or I might expect him to do, but *par en bas,* from underneath. From this subterranean entrance to his home he excavates a runway, or kind of *cloaca maxima,* out to the river; then, in case he should want to make exit to *terra firma* direct, he bores a vertical tunnel from the runway out to the big world above.

It is of this tunnel that I am warning you. For if you be a full-blooded angler, nothing in the world will cure you of watching the running waters as you walk along the river bank. I even hate to suggest that you should abandon for a moment this major joy of angling. "So what?" say you. "So this," say I. As sure as fate, not once but many times as you move stealthily along, all intent upon your lawful occasions, as Patrick Chalmers might say, down into the tunnel will go your advanced leg, not a little way but often right up to your crotch. If you are lucky you will escape with a fright, but you may easily suffer a severe sprain; and, if you be not carrying your rod "at the trail," as all rods should be carried, there is a grim chance of a broken top joint and an end to your day. So I repeat "Beware the beaver hole."

On one occasion on the Madison I fell for the booby trap for the umpteenth time, but this time the Benevolent One "in person" was at the bottom of the tunnel, sitting, like old Caspar, at his cottage door. The commotion and glouglou of thrashing waters which ensued in the *cloaca maxima* scared the wits out of me, so that my leg, which had fallen in, *mirabile dictu,* unharmed, was severely twisted in the exaggerated haste of withdrawal. Bless their hearts, they will have their jokes, these beavers.

And so on, down this lovely river. You cannot fish these ten miles in a day or two days. It will take you many expeditions to learn it all. Some days you will go in below the Barns and work down; other days you will go in at Baker's Hole and work up or down as your mood may dictate. Some evening you will start at the bridge on the Bozeman road and fish down to the muddy flats of the lake bed. Your fish will all run from two to two and a half pounds, with an occasional three-pounder. You won't be worried much, if at all, by small fish. I cannot explain why, for they are there in great numbers. Once at Hole No. 2 I saw a hatch of small fly which suddenly brought to life and activity some two hundred trout up to half a pound, of the existence of which I was totally unaware. The pool was literally alive with them, but often as I have fished it I never saw them in evidence before or since.

At points the river splits round islands. Do not neglect to go round the far sides of these islands; you will find many a beautiful run of water and many a big fish for your trouble. Keep your eye open for points where springs and rivulets come in; there are many of them, and big fish love to lie down-stream of the fresh incoming water. Of the best flies to use I speak later on in this work, so for the moment we will let that ever-present question pass.

Of the Madison below the dam we will treat later, for it is then no longer one of the Four Rivers, but a new river of changed character. So let us pass on to the next of our Four Rivers and see what it offers.

The South Fork

The South Fork reads, in full, South Fork of the Madison. Perhaps before Hebgen was dammed it might have been regarded as such, though it shows a great lack of originality so to name it. As well call the Madison the Middle Fork of the Missouri. A truce to this Fork business, say I. I would like to see the South Fork renamed Crystal Creek, for nowhere in all my wanderings have I seen clearer or more limpid water. Often I have looked down into its depths and thought I was looking at its bed through a magnifying glass. It is incredibly clear, and excessively cold. I know how cold it is, for once, and once only, I followed a fish too far into the South Fork. The pools at its frequent bends are far deeper than one expects or imagines, especially toward its lower end, where the bed is composed largely of volcanic ash, which is easily displaced by the current.

On account of this crystalline character of the water I consider the South Fork to be the most difficult of all the Four Rivers to angle with success. You must make no mistakes on the South Fork; both your art and your artifice must be perfect.

If you wish so to do, you may go up and study it in its early stages where it runs not a foot deep over golden gravel. It is full of interest—to me the origins of all rivers have a fascination—but it is not fishworthy for some miles.

To come to its upper reaches you leave West Yel-

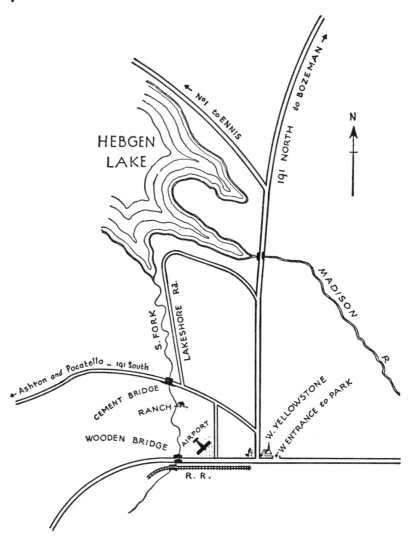

lowstone by continuing down the street which runs
parallel with the railroad, leaving the depot on your
left. In five hundred yards or so, when the road takes
a right-hand swing to join the Ashton road, do not

follow it, but continue along the track straight ahead of you into the fir grove. The airport will lie on your right; in fact the track takes you along its southern boundary and still parallel with the railroad. In a short time you will come to a wooden bridge over the South Fork. Up-stream of this bridge you will find no fish to speak of, but the road follows on up for some miles, if you care to go and study it. Down-stream from the bridge you may fish your happy way. I would not contend that the best fishing is up here, although some Hebgen fish do filter up as far.

The next approach to the river is the cement bridge on the Ashton road, so you may fish this section by starting at the wooden bridge and working down or starting at the cement bridge and working up. It is a long section, and it has an interruption in it. About a mile up-stream from the cement bridge, you will notice a wire fence; this marks the beginning of a ranch which is the property of a New York family who own the rights to both banks for a couple of miles.

You have the right to the bed of the river, but unfortunately, owing to the depth of the pools at the corners, you cannot go far without getting out in order to avoid swimming! I therefore suggest that, in order not to become guilty of trespass, you go to the Ranch House, which is by the waterside, and request the favour of the use of the banks. I myself was met with the greatest courtesy and consideration from the agent in charge, being asked merely to give reasonable clearance to the house and grounds. I subsequently learned how grievously at times the privileges so courteously granted have been abused. I trust that anglers will studiously avoid committing such breaches, because upon the behaviour of one depends the reception of those who come after. Even were that not so, such an appeal calls for no justification.

The beauty of the South Fork at the Ranch and immediately below it, in fact as far as the cement bridge, is to my mind quite exceptional. I tried to catch its intimate loveliness with the camera but signally failed. I have little advice to give you as to how to fish it, for it is fairly obvious, bend after bend, pool after pool. Search out the underhang of the banks, and keep your fish, when hooked, away from the willows, sticks and tree trunks which abound on the deep side. In the evening look for your big strikes, not in the depths of the pools but out on the shallows or ledges, where the big fellows go to feed. But I feel that I am telling you what you know.

One thing you do not know, if you have never fished here before. Avoid fighting the willows. Keep to the water as much as you can, for assuredly the willows are the very deuce. They look weak and pliable but in fact they are as strong as steel. I do not know what made W. S. Gilbert think of the expression "Hey, willow waly oh!" but I could almost think he had fished on the Four Rivers.

I should know the answer to the question, for back in my Oxford days—ye Gods, how long ago—I helped to found a Savoyard Society, probably long since

defunct. I still have among my papers letters from
W. S. G., one accepting the Presidency of our Society
and the other in more Gilbertian vein regretting that
the state of his digestion and the watchful eye of his
wife prevented him from presiding at our annual ban-
quet. He was a savage looking old man, as I remember
him, for he was our friend and neighbour, with shaggy
eyebrows like Tiger Clemenceau and a bark like an
angry dog. He had a reputation for ill temper, but I
fancy it was mostly simulated. The English speaking
world lies certainly very much in his debt.

From the cement bridge on the Ashton road the
river meanders on, still cold, clear and lovely, still
hemmed in by willows, still running over stones worn
smooth by its flow. Not until you get within a few
miles of the lake does its bed commence to change to
black ash. It comes first in little patches piled up on
the stones, then in larger independent patches and
streaks, until finally it takes complete possession.

If you start at the cement bridge, it is far more than
you can do to fish all the way down to the lake in one
day. You must seek closer approach to the lower section. About a hundred yards or so before you come to
the bridge, from the direction of West Yellowstone,
you will notice on your right a dirt road marked "Lake
Shore Road." You will see it shown on my plan. This
road is the key of access to the lower parts of the South
Fork. It runs, as you will see, right up into the angle
of the two southern wings of Hebgen Lake, returning
to the Bozeman road just south of the bridge over the

Madison River. If you follow it you will presently see the South Fork stretched out before you in the valley below. You will find several turnouts where you can park your car; they are well worn by previous anglers. Thus, by approaching it first at the wooden bridge, then at the Ashton road bridge, and lastly from the various points of vantage on the Lake Shore Road, you may make complete acquaintance with as lovely a stream as you could well dream of. Dry fly, wet fly and nymph are all appropriate, according to the mood of the fish, the water and the angler. I have used all three with success.

To be appreciated, the South Fork must be sipped and savoured, not swallowed at a gulp. Taken in this way, it will remain long upon your palate and in your memory. It is a much longer stream than it appears to be, and it will take you many days to become well acquainted with it. But they will be happy days. Even if sometimes you return with an empty creel, which Saint Peter forfend, your heart will be full, full with the peace and the beauty of it all. If you be in tune with the *genius loci* maybe you will hear the pipes of "the great God Pan, down in the reeds by the river." If so, then that night you will be back in the river of your dreams, the water up to your knees, cold and clear, and you with the big one well and truly hooked, slowly coming to safety on the golden gravel beach. And then the pipes of Pan will play again. And what if the pipes prove to be the breakfast bell, and what if your big

If you follow it you will presently see the South Fork stretched out before you in the valley below.

From the bridge on the Ennis Road to the bed of the lake forms the third and last section.

one is awaiting you split and broiled in the dish?
Have you not communed with the Gods?

Grayling Creek

The third of our Four Rivers is the Grayling. It
becomes embarrassing to continue speaking of these
streams in the superlative, but frankly it is the superlative which is called for. I will be as reasonable as I
can. Whilst the run of fish in all the Four Rivers is the
same, the trout of Hebgen, the rivers themselves have
quite different characteristics. The two most similar
in personality are, perhaps, the South Fork and the
Grayling. Yet the Grayling differs within itself, falling naturally into three separate sections, each having
its own personality. The first section runs southward
along the Bozeman road for several miles until it passes
under a bridge, round a bend and out of sight. From
its disappearance at the bridge, until it comes into view
again at the bridge on the Ennis road, it forms another
section, a section in the course of which it becomes a
rocky little torrent and performs considerable gym-
nastics, including a drop over a falls. From the bridge
on the Ennis road to the bed of the lake forms the third
and last section.

The top section does not, I fancy, harbour Hebgen
fish, for I gravely doubt whether many, or even any,
of them get over the falls in the middle of the second
section. Be that as it may, it holds some lovely fish. I

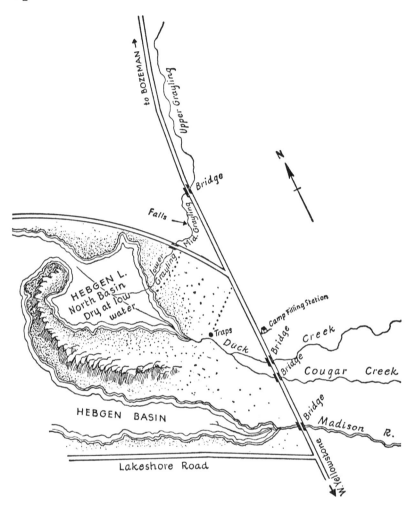

saw one of close upon four pounds brought into Vint Johnson's one evening in July, a beautiful brown in perfect condition, which I regret to say had fallen victim to a live bait. Fish like that are ample evidence of the quality of the water and its food content.

The water of the upper section runs very clear,

though not so diamond clear as the South Fork. The stones and gravel of its bed have a golden tone which makes it peculiarly attractive. Its waters are cold and fast running. Despite its proximity to the road, wild life abounds in this section. I have watched deer standing knee deep in the river in full view of the road and the passers-by. Beavers are the local engineers and keep the dams in good order and the levels up. When I first looked at the upper Grayling I classed it in my mind as a pan fish proposition, but I was a long way from the truth. This upper section is within the Park boundary. In so far as the Park authorities and the State authorities do not necessarily coincide in the opening and closing dates allotted to waters under their respective cares, be careful to make sure that the river is open when you fish it. It is so accessible from the road, with a number of excellent turnouts for your convenience, that I do not need to add much. A great many grayling were planted in the upper Grayling this summer, so in the near future the prospects of some excellent grayling fishing are good. This is a very popular run of water, so do not expect to have it to yourself, especially at week-ends. Take a short rod, for it is not a wide water and it is well hedged in. You will probably lose a fly or two, but you won't be able to stay out of temper for long in such perfect surroundings.

The middle section, which runs through the canyon, is not quite so easy. It may, as already explained, be approached from the Bozeman road at the top end or from the Ennis road at the bottom end. I know of no other approach. If you wish to approach it from below, you take the Ennis road (which branches to the left off the Bozeman road about ten miles out of West Yellowstone), and about a quarter of a mile before you get to the bridge over the Grayling you will see a dirt road, or track, running both to the right and to the left. Take off to the right, and in a very short distance you will come to a wooden bridge, across which, on your right-hand side, is a large sheltering tree under which you may park. From here you work your way up-stream.

You will first be greeted with a lovely stretch of water that comes down past some byres and farm buildings. As you work on up, the bed becomes rougher and more slippery and the pace of the stream faster. The woods beside the river take on, at this point, a particular beauty. In June the wild flowers make a riot of colour. Wild life is abundant. It was here that a friend from my camp took flight from a moose. I don't blame him, especially as he already had a good catch. It was here also that my Sealyham terrier, Flappie, was put to complete rout by a pair of ruffed grouse defending their brood. Very menacing they looked with their tails spread, heads low and hackles up. They were strange enemies to Flappie; so taking, according to the dictum, *omne ignotum pro horrifico,* she forsook the field.

I might at this juncture say a word about my pal.

You will, I hope, find her picture amongst the illustrations to this work. She has been my constant companion on this and many another trip; for, *entre nous*, she is now an old lady of five summers. Despite her years, however, she still believes in keeping gay and ridiculous, and her antics are a constant source of enjoyment to me. Everything is fun to her. All furred animals, from chipmunks to bears, are classed as "mousies," a word the merest whisper of which sets her into a palsy of excitement, and a fury of barking and simulated rage. But she doesn't mean the half of what she barks. She sticks it through the longest and hottest days, half lost in the high grass, falling into beaver holes, getting carried away down-stream, just one adventure after another. Only once was she licked, on the trek out from the Bechler River. For the last mile I had to carry her, I almost as beat as she was. She tried to tell me "I just hate to have you do this, but I simply can't go another yard." No, Sir, I would not part with her for all the gold in Fort Knox.

But to return to our river; presently you realize that you are working up into a gorge. If you are young and agile, you will go on and in due course you will come out at the bridge on the Bozeman road, the foot of the first section. You will find good fishing as you go, in rough, fast water. Your tackle must be in good order, for the pace of the stream will add vastly to the pull of your trout. Wear either nails or felt on your soles, for the bottom is infernally slippery and a dis-

abling fall in this out-of-the-way region would be unpleasant.

Let us see what we come to if we start from the other
end, the bridge on the Bozeman road. For the first few
hundred yards the character of the upper reach is
maintained, but gradually you will observe a tendency
to change. A long straight run faces us, peculiarly long
and straight for these waters. It is still willow-screened
on the right, with a large meadow behind the screen;
but on the left there rises a sheer fir-clad slope. If you
happen ever to have been to Wildbad in the Black
Forest and fished the Enz, you will at this spot see it
all over again. I wonder who fishes those waters now.
I read recently that Germany discourages foreign anglers, but nothing surprises me any longer about that
distracted land.

A little further, and the land to your right begins to
rise; the river bed becomes rocky and rough, and the
golden stones disappear. You are being prepared mentally for a change, the full significance of which is soon
upon you. You look up and see that you are gradually
being hemmed in on both sides by rocky heights. The
river becomes a succession of swirling pools. The "Prix
de Chamois" now begins. Since I suffer from an old
football injury to my knee, and am further blessed, or
should I say cursed, with a measure of natural cau-
tion, I beg to be excused from entering the race. I am
told that the falls in mid-canyon are very beautiful.
If you continue on, you will see them and will meet
that other self whom we left wending his way up from

below. You can then compare notes with him. You must write and tell me all about it! Tell me in particular how you handle the situation from your rocky perch when the big fellow takes you and beats it down-stream through a series of miniature Niagaras with your pet fly in his nose. "Tell me, tell me all about it." I shall be interested to hear.

The third and last stretch, though not big water, **is** big fishing. I at least have caught more large fish in the bottom section of the Grayling than in either the South Fork or the Duck, and as many, I fancy, as in the Madison. In between the runs of spawning fish, it does not afford so much sport with "inhabitants" as the Madison. It does not have the same cover or the same food, and therefore cannot compete with the Madison as a realtor in the leasing of permanent trout abodes. But in the spring and fall, when they are running, it certainly does provide wonderful sport.

The approach is from the bridge on the Ennis road; but, in so far as it is a long stretch, when the lake is low you need to be able to drive further down, so as to avoid long tramps to and from your angling. You remember the right and left track just before you get to the bridge? You took the right-hand one in order to go up the centre section. Well, this time you take the left one. Go slow, for it leads you over a bump or two, and in and out of willow clumps which cover up your visibility ahead of you. It will take you down to the riverside and away out into the marshland which at high water becomes lake. If the weather has been wet, do not risk it, for you will assuredly get stuck; and even if it be dry, park on a high and dry spot near the wheel tracks. You may meet with sudden electric storms down in the basin. These storms are of short duration, but they are so violent that you may have a job to get under way again when homeward bound. I got caught once in this manner, and had to send fifteen miles into West Yellowstone for a pull out. I was only ten or fifteen yards off the beaten track, but I couldn't make them under my own power for love or money.

What a storm that one was! It reversed all my old beliefs about the habits of fish and the theory that thunder puts them down. It opened with a sudden icy blast blowing up-valley in my face; then the rain, cold, hard, relentless; then thunder and lightning that seemed to split the very earth and sky. In a second I was drenched to the skin. I could not get any wetter, so I decided to fish on. Shortening my line I proceeded to punch my fly into the gale. Now a gale in my face makes a bad-tempered man out of me, for I have great difficulty in driving a fly into the wind. (I told you that I am only in the second class as an angler.) I was wondering why I was stupid enough to go on when, of a sudden, bang, I was taken, and by a good fish too. For over an hour the storm raged, and the more it raged the faster the fish took. Rainbows, browns and even whitefish, they all took, and took madly. I thought it must be a dream and I should wake up. I put on my largest salmon fly; even that the whitefish took, though how they got it into their stupid looking mouths I do not know. It was the "blue moon" that all anglers live for and dream of. I ceased to count how many fish I caught and returned to the water. Two rainbows which I kept turned the scales later at near three pounds apiece. Then suddenly the storm ceased, as suddenly as it had commenced. Out came the sun again, down went the fish and all the excitement of that hectic hour passed away like a dream. Wet but happy I made my way back to the car, and it was only then that I learned what a sudden storm can do to an already marshy soil, and why I am warning you. Perhaps you will reply that on those conditions you would welcome a spot of storm yourself!

The last two or three miles of the Grayling in the marshes are somewhat bare and grim. The willows have all been rotted down by the water to dry sticks, which make the banks look a veritable golgotha. These dried-up willow sticks are bad enough around you, catching your line or your fly at any opportunity offered and holding it as in a vice. In the river bed they are worse, for they are a boon to the hooked fish, who will use them to your discomfiture, if you let him. He will tie you up in them, then disengage himself and lie under the bank chuckling while he watches you "play" the willow stick. If it be a lissome one, it can fool you through long minutes of spurious excitement, with its give and take, its tremulous tugs, until you could swear it was a trout. Once in the English Wye I played a strand of submerged wire in mistake for a salmon for over half an hour!

Duck Creek

In his excellent book *Fishing Round the World,* Leander McCormick has a chapter entitled "River Test, Test River." I know Leander well enough to plagiarize first and apologize afterwards. "Duck Creek, duck of a creek," say I, and I mean it. That just describes it, this Benjamin of our little family of four.

In the Duck I include, as previously stated, the Cougar. It comes down from the Park, across the Bozeman road under its own private bridge, and joins the Duck a mile or more, riverwise, above the traps. The Cougar is smaller than the Duck, which itself is a small river; it has no special features which call for differentiation or separate treatment, but it offers several miles of good, if somewhat confined, fishing.

The higher reaches of the Duck lie within the Park, running for many miles through woods and meadows. I have never fished these reaches, since unfortunately during my visit they were closed to fishing, owing to a series of forest fires in this region which were attributed to anglers. I have, however, walked some way up it, and it has all the appearance of a perfect dry fly stream. The Hebgen fish run up it, and I am informed by the trappers that they pick up just as fine fish in the traps on the Duck as they do in those on the Madison and the South Fork.

The Duck has one outstanding point of variation from the other members of the Big Four. Its bed is not of stone or gravel, at least not visibly so, but of mud.

. . . my constant companion on this and many another trip . . . No, Sir,
I would not part with her for all the gold in Fort Knox.

*The higher reaches of the Duck lie within the Park, running for many miles
through woods and meadows.*

Of course below the mud there must be a hard base, but there is a considerable mud accretion. I would imagine that this is due to slower pace and more gradual fall, preventing the mud from being carried down to the lake. In consequence its waters, whilst being clear in themselves, do not appear to be clear and limpid like the others. However, the Duck is a stream of great charm. From the bridge on the Bozeman road right down to where it runs into the Grayling in the bed of Hebgen Lake, it has the standard twisting willow-edged character, the same deep pools at the bends, the same runs and riffles and cast-up ledges.

Above the Bozeman road, however, it changes. It has more straight runs and flat water. Up-stream of the beaver dam it runs for a while with the stillness of a canal. Here among the weeds lie big fish which only appear in the evening when the fly is on the water. The weeds are too near the surface for a wet fly; you must fish dry, but you must make your first cast an accurate one. The prevalent weed is a flowing one with a white starlike flower; it reminds me of the *ranunculus fluitans* of the streams of southern England, and in particular of the Chess where Frank Pither, to his everlasting credit, first induced me to take up angling.

Alas, today our old haven of peace has fallen to the builder. I wonder whose garden plot now runs down to the corner where I caught my first sizable fish. The may-fly was up; it was duffers' delight for ten glorious days. When he hit me I let off a whoop which brought Jo and Frank along at the double. I was boot-high in the stream, tense and determined, every nerve on strain. Advice flowed freely but kindly, prompted only by affection and the fear that I might lose my prize. Under the strain of the battle I took it ill; I snapped back, rudely, asking whose the hell fish was it anyway. How we laughed afterwards when my two-pounder lay safe on the bank. *Eheu, fugaces!* Are there not tears indeed in looking back on the days and the dear ones that are gone beyond recall?

So if some evening you sense in the air conditions propitious to an evening rise, take your lightest rod, a leader tapered to three, and a selection of dry flies, and make your way up the Duck from the bridge on the Bozeman road. You will have a full evening's entertainment before you reach the Park boundary. Your first chance of a good fish will probably present itself just below or above the old wooden bridge by the house where the dog barks at you. Do not turn up your nose at the shallowness of the water. On the shallows is where the fish will be feeding, so go warily, or you will suddenly see the wake of a torpedo and your chance gone until tomorrow. Remember, this is a stalking proposition.

On your left at this point there is a floating bog of horrible jellified consistency. Avoid it as you would the devil, or those who come to seek you may learn of your passing only by the evidence of the top few feet of your rod sticking up in silent testimony to an angler gone west in line of duty! Even so do the bayo-

*. . . it has the standard twisting willow-edged character, the same deep pools
at the bends, the same runs and riffles and cast-up ledges.*

Nothing in animal motion is as unexpected as the gracefulness of a moose in movement.

nets of a gallant little company still protrude from the soil of Douaumont, grim memorial to as heroic an episode as was ever lived through and died through in all those four years of tragic imbecility. They were no vain boast, those immortal words, *"Ils ne passeront pas."*

Avoiding, then, the trembling bog, you will fish on with varying luck until you come to the beaver dam. Here you should surely get a good fish in the pool which the Benevolent One has so carefully engineered for you. You will also probably fall into one of his booby traps, for he has set many around here. Above the dam you will come to the long still stretch; there lie the best fish of the evening. You must lie in wait for them, and the mosquitoes love a waiting angler; but it's well worth it if you catch a brace.

Some other day you will tackle the Duck from the Bozeman road downwards. This will be more than you can manage in one expedition. There is a natural "half way house" at the traps. If you climb the wooden steps up to the trapper's hut on the bluff, you can make your way straight out across the sage brush to the Ennis road. There swing right and you come back to where you left your car. You will observe that the track from the trapper's hut to the road is quite driveable, so, on the next trip, when you fish from the traps down to the lake, you can make the trapper's hut your parking place.

Any attempt to get out from the Duck through the willows spells trouble. I tried it once. I made for the fir wood on the left, which I reached dishevelled and panting but still in good order. Then I set my course light-heartedly in the general direction of the Bozeman road. I had by now quite forgotten the existence of the intervening Cougar, whose confluence I had in fact observed as I passed it some hours back. In due course I found myself in the willows again, this time the willows of the Cougar. Then suddenly I heard a crash and a splash. There, thought I, is some unfortunate angler fallen head first into the stream. Without further ado I hurried forward, parted the final curtain of willows, and found myself looking into the muzzle of the world's largest bull moose.

Now the face of a big moose on the wall of a club smoking-room or in the pleasant distance of the meadows, with a river running between, is positively benign; but, at hot-breath distance, the face of a moose disturbed at his morning drink is a very ugly affair. For, I suppose, thirty seconds—or was it really thirty minutes?—we looked each other in the eye disapprovingly. Then out of sheer fear and embarrassment I broke the unbearable silence by some fatuous remark. Luckily this decided him that I was not worth bothering about, or we might still have been there trying to stare each other out of countenance. With a disdainful lift of his great head and a long easy swing, he leaped out of the river and past me at a bound. Nothing in animal motion is as unexpected as the gracefulness of a moose in movement. All its stationary ungainliness becomes transformed into beauty, rhythm and grace. And was I glad to see him go!

You will probably see more wild life as you wander down the Duck than you will on any of the other rivers. That, at least, is my experience. One feels peculiarly sheltered on the Duck, and I fancy that the birds and beasts feel it too. The birds are there in hundreds; ducks, of course, are there, for where else should you look for them but on Duck Creek? Happily, by the same analogy, you are not likely to meet any cougars on the Cougar; an occasional moose is more than enough. I have sat there watching cranes, herons, bitterns, hawks and many birds whose names I know not, for hour upon hour. Somehow the Duck makes me contemplative. I never fish it as hard as I do the other rivers, I can't say why. When first I saw it I was not greatly attracted, but as I have come to know it, it has grown upon me, so that now I have a particular and personal affection for it. I recommend it to you with all my heart.

CHAPTER SIX

ABOUT OTHER RIVERS

THE next honours are due, I feel, to the Yellowstone River. It is by far the largest and most important river in the Park and it is the home of the cutthroat trout. When I say "it" I am referring to that section of it which runs northward out of the lake at Fishing Bridge and away through the Canyon to Gardiner and "all points north."

The part of the Yellowstone River which I would dearly love to see and to fish is that part which runs from the south boundary of the Park into the lake at the southeastern arm, for this lies up-stream of the base depot and therefore should be filled every spring with fat trout running up in search of spawning beds. It is not trapped, presumably on account of its size; therefore, there is no record of what it may or may not contain, such as a trapper's report might give you. It is accessible only by motor boat or by pack-horse. Either of these trips is a comparatively expensive trip, and the latter is lengthy. You remember what Al Smith said about his recent trip to Europe—that he had been trying all his life to make it, that sometimes he had had the time but not the money, other times the money but not the time? Well, it's like that with me and angling, only mostly it is the money that is lacking and

When I say "it" I am referring to that section of it which runs northward out of the lake at Fishing Bridge . . .

Except for a big bend near the Mud Geyser, it runs beside the river all the way from Fishing Bridge to Canyon . . .

not the time. However, Al made it, so why shouldn't I some day see the upper Yellowstone River?

I have spoken with Rangers about it. On the whole they have a tendency to discourage the suggestion, saying that the fishing is nothing to write home about and that it is a very uncomfortable trip. I have a sneaking suspicion that Rangers acquire over the years a kind of proprietary sense about their hinterlands, almost a jealousy which makes them discourage invasion. I once suggested that some day a road will probably be built all around Yellowstone Lake, but I was quickly made to feel that I was talking heresy. Smith and Kendall state, in their document already referred to: "Above the lake the Yellowstone River winds through marshy meadows between wooded hills, behind which are the rugged peaks of high volcanic mountains. The current is sluggish and according to Mr. Dinsmore the fall is so slight that it would be a comparatively easy matter in times of ordinary flow to travel by canoe the entire distance from the lake to the southern boundary of the Park." If any reader has done this trip and would care to let me know what the fishing was like, I would be grateful for the information. I still cannot but think that some great cutthroats are to be found there, though it may be that the wish is father to the thought.

We must then leave the upper river to the imagination, and to the day when we have both the time and the money, and come to the lower one. Once more the road is your friend. Except for a big bend near the Mud Geyser, it runs beside the river all the way from

Fishing Bridge to Canyon; and that really comprises the fishable water, with the exception of a stretch of heavy water near Tower Junction, to which I will refer later. After Canyon it becomes too much of torrent for the average angler, too dangerous and with too little reward. In the heavy rivers of Germany, Austria and Yugoslavia (excellent angling country, the latter) they fish turgid waters in safety by wearing a belt with a steel ring attached and having a life-line tied to the ring and held by a gillie. That is the gear you require if you want to fish the Yellowstone down in the canyon. Once I did, at the instigation of a young acquaintance, clamber down below the falls and fish precariously from a rock. Strange to say, against all my expectations and prophecies, I did catch some trout; but they were no bigger or better than those which I caught with greater ease in the normal reaches of the river, and the return journey up the canyon side was a pain in the small of the back. So let us be normal folks and fish where the river is accessible and practicable.

Even there it is a powerful river, running clear and swift over a bed of large stones, so do not over-estimate your strength when wading it. At times and in places there crop up through the stones patches and layers of white clay. This white clay is as slippery as the Cresta Run, and if you tread upon it unwarily it is all Lombard Street to a blood orange that you will a-swimming go.

I did so once when I was wading back across the river at the big pool below the Road Workers' camp. I was carrying a proud catch of four beauties, for which I had risked all to get to the other side where the better fish lie. Almost within reach of shore my foot hit the clay. Away I went in a flash, feet up, body in the cold water, and rod and parcel of fish gone widdershins. The paper of the parcel unfolded in the water like a lily pad, and the last I saw of my four beauties they were still afloat, being carried down on the face of the waters like some offering to the Gods of the River. My balance I recovered after a short swim and my rod at the next bend in the stream. Now I watch out for white patches in the bed of the Yellowstone River.

You can see, as you travel along the road from Lake Junction, where the fishing conveniently begins. There is a spit of gravel running out into the stream and there are generally two or three anglers in command of that strategic point. Personally I am not of the stand-still school in wet fly work. I move slowly, but I move, trying to cover my water as I go.

It is a mighty river, not intimate like the four friends we have been discussing in the last chapter. If you can take in a good third of its width, you are not casting badly. It is to me a thousand pities that there is not a bridge about half way between Fishing Bridge and Canyon. It would distribute the anglers and double the available water. A foot bridge would suffice. There is, as I have indicated, one point at which I have got over late in the season, but it is nip and tuck and not the kind of wading I would like to recommend. I do not know what objection there may be, or whether, if there be an objection other than cost, it is insuperable; but I do believe that the idea of a bridge is one of merit.

There is not in truth a great deal that I can advise you about fishing the Yellowstone River. It is all very self-evident. There is one spot where there is a remarkable dry fly rise almost every evening, which is, perhaps, worth calling to your attention in case you miss it. This is one of the rare spots where almost every evening the trout come and dine like gentlemen upstairs, where a definite "rise," as against an occasional rising fish, may be observed. Just up-stream from the Mud Geyser you will see on the left of the roadside an inscribed board relating something of the exploits of one General Howard. Eight tenths of a mile further up-stream from this board you will come to a spot where the river rejoins the road after a temporary absence. There is a little lone fir tree by the water's edge, and an island, or peninsula, I forget which, in the stream to your left. About five o'clock in the evening wade across the backwater to the peninsula and watch up-stream. Unless things have changed from what they used to be, you will presently see the commencement of a rise. At first it will be the smaller fish rising on your right about twenty feet out from the edge of the stream. Then further out in the stream the bigger ones will take it up, until finally they are boiling all around you. With long waders you can get out just far enough to reach the bigger fish with a good cast. The smaller ones are fairly easy; I have caught many of them and

It is a mighty river . . .

She is full of strength, this new Madison; she is not unkind, she means no harm, but she is in a great hurry and will sweep away anything which impedes her progress.

so will you. But the big ones, no, Sir. I have tried all I know how—dry flies, nymphs, floating leader, sunken leader—all the tricks I know, but to no avail. So there is the wise word for the experts; there are fish that will be a match for them.

On the down-stream side of the Mud Geyser (you will know it by its smell), the river smooths out for miles through flat meadows. Here of an evening, and often for that matter through the day, you will see fish constantly rising and fishermen wielding hopeful rods. I think I have seen more novices in this stretch than anywhere. I once saw one employing the most unique method of casting that has ever come to my notice. He extended his line along the ground, then whirled it around in the air, himself pirouetting the while, like an athlete throwing the hammer; then, when the psychologic moment came (I don't know how he recognized it), he suddenly directed the whole motion out riverwards, only just managing to refrain from following it in person and making a sub-aqueous inspection of the result. It was magnificent, but it was not exactly standard practice.

You could fish the Yellowstone River for a long time without tiring of it, and certainly without conquering it. It has many lessons to teach, and it is essentially a water where good casting pays.

The last mile or so before Canyon does not seem, for some inscrutable reason, to hold fish. I have never seen anyone fishing between the side road which leads to the bear-feeding ground and the bridge. I once tried

it, out of curiosity, and never had a touch; admittedly
not a searching experiment, but, such as it was, it
seemed to confirm the general verdict.

There is one expedition which you might well make
and that is to the Yellowstone River at Tower Junction. Here there is a stretch of heavy fast water which
I have been told holds good fish. It certainly looks as
though it should. It faces you down in the valley as you
look across the barrier in front of the car park. I fished
it once, but a previous engagement did not permit of
my staying till evening, and I think that, for the big
ones, if indeed they are there, the evening is the only
time. I did catch quite a number of small and medium
fish, somewhat to my surprise, but that was not what
I was looking for.

Lower Madison

And now I suddenly remember that I cut you off
from our good Madison River at Hebgen, promising
to follow it further at a later stage. I think that moment has come, so let us go to the far end of Hebgen
(you know the way, along the Ennis road) and watch
the new Madison, now four-in-one, pour out from under the sluices into its new rocky bed, sole nominee of
the waters. It now becomes a swift-flowing, powerful
river, a little conceited perhaps at having played so
vital a part in the creation of power for the use of
mankind. Between the sluices and the wooden bridge
you may not fish; you must grant it this short distance

to settle down and find itself; but beyond the wooden bridge it is yours to coax, or whip or flog for miles and miles and miles. I have never followed it beyond Ennis, and that, if I remember right, is some sixty miles. I recall that the folk of Ennis claimed that only within their boundaries did it attain perfection, but to keep within the reasonable scope of this unpretentious work I do not propose to take you so far afield, nor to enter into arguments as to who has the best of it. Were I to do so, we might find ourselves fighting it out with the folk of Omaha or Paducah, and eventually listening to the claims of the Mississippi Valley folk as the rightful claimants to the fine trout which have been swept down by the floods. A reasonable and appropriate barrier would be the bridge at Hutchins, which is some twelve miles down-stream from Hebgen, though nothing prevents you from going further, should you feel so inclined.

The next bridge, after the wooden bridge below the dam, is another wooden bridge that spans the river about seven miles down-stream. This new Madison is much too large a river to cover from one bank, and, unless the sluices be severely constricted, is for the most part too deep and rough to cross on foot. Therefore make up your mind which bank you will fish, for your twelve miles are in fact twenty-four potential miles of fishing down to Hutchins. I repeat that the rate of release of water from the dam makes a vast difference to this fishing. I have seen the Madison below the dam three feet above its banks and I have seen it sneaking along like a guilty school-boy; in general, however, my representation of it as a powerful river should hold correct.

This, curiously enough, is the one stretch of water in the Yellowstone area where I got the impression that the use of the right fly is of importance. Above the lake I would confidently suggest half a dozen patterns, any one of which, properly presented, would upon any day take fish; but below Hebgen it seems to be another matter. They are probably wary from much fishing, these inhabitants, and also less in a hurry than the running spawners who have an urgent duty to perform and cannot bother to stop too long and think.

All along the river runs our friend the road, so that you may spend a day fishing, now here, now there, as the fancy seizes you. Wade carefully, especially in places where you have not been before. She is full of strength, this new Madison; she is not unkind, she means no harm, but she is in a great hurry and will sweep away anything which impedes her progress.

Lamar and Soda Butte

You have already found the way to Tower Junction. It is a lovely road from Canyon to Tower, well made and graded, with gorgeous views. If you go on a little way beyond Tower Junction, you will come to Roosevelt Camp. Here the Cooke Mountain road swings off to the right, leading you to the northeast exit of the Park. This, incidentally, is one of the loveliest scenic

You will pass over the Yellowstone River, now a torrent of green and blue waters . . .

For some few miles the road runs alongside of it . . .

Then, near the Soda Butte Ranger Station, you see the Soda Butte come to join it. It is now the Soda Butte which the road parallels.

The Lamar can be seen away to the right, wending its way down from the Absaroka mountains.

routes in all America, and, fishing or no fishing, you should take a day to ride along it to Red Lodge, Montana. With the exception of the first few miles, it is beautifully graded, a perfect modern highway, with no harsh gradients, despite the height to which it climbs.

The first few miles after the take-off from the Tower road are tortuous, so drive slowly. You will pass over the Yellowstone River, now a torrent of green and blue waters, and in a mile or so you will come to the bridge over the Lamar, coming down through the valley to your right on its way to join the Yellowstone. Right there above the bridge it looks, and is, most fishable. For some few miles the road runs alongside of it, so you may study it and take your choice. Then, near the Soda Butte Ranger Station, you see the Soda Butte come to join it. It is now the Soda Butte which the road parallels. The Lamar can be seen away to the right, wending its way down from the Absaroka mountains. From its origin up there it travels many miles to meet the Soda Butte by the roadside. If you want to get to know it, you must take a pack-horse and follow it. I am told that the fishing is good, but in stormy weather the upper reaches of the Lamar become very coloured. I have seen it running like pea soup right down to its confluence with the Soda Butte, and then continuing as one river with a line of division clear down the centre, one half gin, one half pea soup.

As for the Soda Butte, it is a pretty stream but, running as it does along a main highway and having no lake from which to draw fresh fish, it becomes fished out very early in the season, so if you cannot fish it in June, do not bother to fish it at all, except in the last two weeks of July. At about this period the Soda Butte, for the first mile or so above its junction with the Lamar, is apt to offer first-class dry fly fishing.

You will remember that near here is Fish Lake, so do not forget to call on the Ranger and have him take you up there. An hour's time will suffice for the trip up and back, even less if you only take a hurried view; but once there I fancy you will want to linger awhile. Before you drive away take a look at the knob of old geyser accretion on the other side of the road. On the far side of it you will find a busy colony of rock swallows flitting in and out of their neatly constructed homes.

Slough Creek

As you rode along from the bridge over the Lamar River to Soda Butte, you may have noticed, if you are observant, a dirt road which takes off to the left and a sign which says "To Slough Creek." Slough, I may remark, is locally pronounced as though it was written Sloo. This is an important turning, for it leads you to a first-class day's dry fly fishing. I say dry fly, but wet fly will do if, like many that I have met, you think there is some mystery or special difficulty about dry fly fishing. You may be sure of your road by noting a letter-box on a pole, looking somewhat like a large deserted dove-cot. You follow this dirt road for two miles or so, ignoring all spurs which run off to the left

Before you drive away take a look at the knob of old geyser accretion on the other side of the road. On the far side of it you will find a busy colony of rock swallows flitting in and out of their neatly constructed homes.

*You follow this dirt road for two miles or so, ignoring all spurs which run off
to the left and lead down to the river which you can see in the valley below you.*

The meadows where the big fish are to be found lie two or three miles up-stream, and the route by way of the river is rocky and arduous, fit only for mountain goats.

If you proceed very quietly about the business in hand, Mr. and Mrs. Wood-
chuck may be induced to come out from under and join you in a little fruit,
chirruping with a mixture of greed and fear, their funny grey whiskers
a-twitch and their glowing brown coats all fluffy and bright.

and lead down to the river which you can see in the valley below you. For it is not on this visible section that I want to take you fishing.

The meadows where the big fish are to be found lie two or three miles up-stream, and the route by way of the river is rocky and arduous, fit only for mountain goats. Elderly sportsmen like myself, who are going gently down the westering slope of life, will do better to follow my more cautious lead. So for that matter will youthful anglers, for I once heard a young college giant say "Never again" upon his return from that expedition over the rocks. So continue along the road until you come to a sign labelled "Vehicles Excluded," just short of a log cabin on the left.

Here you park the car in what shade you can find and make ready for a forty-minute trek up the trail which faces you. The initial grade is tough, so do not carry more gear than you need. Rubber boots are sufficient for the wading ahead of you, so you had better put them on now. Sling your gear over your shoulder, for you will need one hand to carry your rod and the other to fight off the mosquitoes. After the first half mile the trail flattens out and becomes easier. At the end of some thirty or forty minutes, according to your form and fitness, "round a bend of a sudden" you will see the river winding through the meadows, as welcome to your weary view as was the sight of the sea to the Macedonian soldiers of old, as they raised a shout of *"Thalatta! Thalatta!"* By one of memory's queer quirks they came back to my mind at this moment out of the school-boy mists of more than forty years ago.

Right there in the meadows you will find a Ranger Station and an obliging Ranger who will inform you that the fishing is good all through the meadows up to the wooden bridge, more than enough to keep you busy for the day. He will also inform you that if you care to work your way on up through the next five miles or so of broken water you will come to the upper meadows, which also afford great fishing, and which, needless to say, are very much less fished. I took the upper meadows on faith, for sufficient unto the day is the trek thereof. If ever I see those upper meadows it will, I fear, only be from the windows of heaven.

Before starting to fish, tiffin is indicated. Just short of the Ranger Station there is a large rock which will serve excellently for seats and table. If you proceed very quietly about the business in hand, Mr. and Mrs. Woodchuck may be induced to come out from under and join you in a little fruit, chirruping with a mixture of greed and fear, their funny grey whiskers a-twitch and their glowing brown coats all fluffy and bright. But you must keep still, almost motionless, or you will lose them; and then to get them back needs more patience than ever.

There are plenty of really large cutthroats in Slough Creek. Three-pounders create no excitement. The water is excessively clear and the surface slow moving. When I saw it it was covered with out-size bugs of the grasshopper order, and the fish I caught and killed were full of them. I should think an imitation grasshopper would be an excellent lure to take along with you. You will find that it pays to tack from side to side of the stream as you go, always keeping to the shallow shelving side and casting across under the bank where the water runs deep.

You will surely pass a happy day, far from the crowd. Toward dusk you will take the trail back to your waiting car. If, as may well happen, there be a four-pounder in your creel, the lightness of your heart will balance out the weight of your load, and I wouldn't be surprised if Mr. and Mrs. Woodchuck did not hear the refrain of some old happy tune come humming to them across the stillness as you pass up the hill into the falling night.

Cache Creek

By the way, I omitted to tell you, when visiting the Ranger at Soda Butte, to ask him the way up to Cache Creek. The Cache is a tributary of the Lamar. The trail runs off at the lone tree below the Station and takes you four miles up into the hills to where lie the skeletons of some grizzlies, apparently overcome by geyser emanations. Here you will find excellent fishing, but for smaller fish. You probably won't get one over a pound, but there will be lots of them for you and a day full of fun.

Clear Creek

Another day with a slight trek to it, which I forgot to mention, is back by Yellowstone Lake beyond Fishing Bridge. Take the Cody road toward the east entrance to the Park. Just at the point where the road leaves the lake shore, you will see a trail to your right. This is the long trail which runs all along the lake as far as the southern section of the Yellowstone River, the trail to the South Yellowstone River which some day I hope to take when time and money coincide. Don't be frightened. I am not going to suggest a forty-mile hike. Two miles is all that I want you to travel now, until you come to where Clear Creek runs into the lake. Here is really good fishing; you should catch a big fish or two here, and on a dry fly, if that amuses you.

The Gallatin River

Now I must take you out of the Park again, out by the western gate and along our old friend, the Bozeman road. We run on past the upper reach of the Grayling, stoutly resisting the temptation to stop once more by its golden waters and throw a line. Not long after we lose the Grayling we see another river wending its way toward us through the meadows to the right. What a country of running waters! In but a few miles' run along the Bozeman road, we have passed over the Madison, the Cougar, the Duck, the Grayling, and now we come to the Gallatin, which is to be our friend and companion for most of the next fifty miles or so.

It looks all young and fresh and innocent when we first see it, but in point of fact it has already travelled some fifteen miles from its source in little Gallatin

Lake, away up in the hinterland of the Park. From the Park boundary at the road it passes into the care of the Gallatin National Forest. I have never fished the Park section up to the source, although I have been fired with tales of green meadows and great fish. Equally, however, I have been told to give it a miss. I neither believe nor disbelieve. I know how I have sung the praises of a golf course when, on a rare occasion, I have shot an eighty. Yet what an infamous and ill-designed mud heap it can become when those dastardly figures add up to nigh a hundred. Circumstances alter cases; they also alter opinions. If ever I were fortunate enough to return, with leisure ahead of me, to the delectable land of which I am writing, I would hire me a horse for the further study of these outlying places. No, I would not fish from a-back the nag, though that too is a good old Spanish custom. I would tether him whilst I fished afoot, and I would use him to ford the difficult places, and, oh, would he be welcome at the end of the day!

The Gallatin is a great and famous river. It is, as I have pointed out, one of the triumvirate which join forces to form the Missouri River. For a mile or two from the time we meet it until we espy the Ranger Station on our left it seems content to pursue a quiet course; we even might think of a dry fly toward the evening hour. But before long it changes both its mind and its character. It develops a grey quality, presumably from the inflow of creeks coming down from the high mountains where snow still lies. These mountain tributaries are numerous. Its surface becomes rough, first at the bends alone, and then gradually all along its length. Its trout are strong and hardy, though many of them are small. There is a big body of fish of some half to three quarters of a pound, mostly rainbows. These are bred in the many creeks which feed the Gallatin, and you will catch them all the time.

Of course it is the big ones you will be hoping for. There are many of them, but they are frankly hard to catch. The local folk catch the large "salmon flies," as they call them, dragon-flies in my parlance (they are really large stone flies, *pteronarcys californica*) and impale them upon weighted hooks, and then sink them down to the bottom of the pools where they suspect the large fish to lie. From time to time they are successful, but personally I prefer the artifice of a salmon fly proper, as spoken of on the Dee or the Tweed, an honest and cunning concoction of many-hued feathers deftly tied to a good heavy hook. The Gallatin is so long that I recommend, if on first experience it tempts you, that you stay a few days at Karst's Camp, about 35 miles out of West Yellowstone. You will be in the centre of the good fishing; you will be comfortable and well cared for on reasonable terms.

Many of the tributaries to which I have referred afford good sport if you hike a little way up from their junctions and seek the more secluded spots. One which is of especially good report is Fan Creek, which slips away to the right very soon after you meet the Gallatin and runs catty corner across the northwest corner of

The Gallatin is a great and famous river.

One which is of especially good report is Fan Creek, which slips away to the right very soon after you meet the Gallatin and runs catty corner across the northwest corner of the Park.

the Park.

The Gallatin can never be fished out, like the smaller rivers of which I have told you. It has too much water, too many hiding places and too many fish. Therefore it is good ground for late July and early August, when the other rivers have been fished hard and the fresh run of spawning fish has not commenced.

The Widow's Preserve

The last water of which I am going to talk to you in any detail is one around which hangs a little tale and a modicum of mystery. The little tale I will tell you. The mystery is the mystery of location. I solved it for myself and will leave you to do likewise if the spirit moves you.

When I became in 1936 a frenzied seeker after knowledge about angling possibilities in the West, a friend of my daughter was lunching with us one day and suggested that I ring up her father. I did so and was cordially invited to come and have a talk over a whisky and soda. After appropriate preliminaries, the gentleman informed me that he had once been up fishing around Yellowstone with a friend. His own experiences, he said, were comparatively uneventful. There was something he could tell me, however, about his friend which perhaps I might turn to account. Every now and then this friend would disappear at break of day, leaving a note that he would not return until late. On these occasions he would invariably come home carrying a catch of stupendous trout. Nothing, however, would drag from him the whereabouts of the prolific waters which yielded up such beauties, but they were somewhere sufficiently within reach of West Yellowstone to be fishable in a day's trip.

Such was the exiguous but exciting information which was kindly vouchsafed to me that evening over a whisky and soda in the comfort of a Houston home. I will not tell you of all the trouble I took to locate the spot, but locate it I did.

The site of the story is a farm lying up in a valley among the hills of Montana. The country around reminds me of Scotland in its austerity and cold beauty; reminds me of Cauldstaneslap as Stevenson describes it in *Weir of Hermiston*.

Back about 1870 the farm was purchased by a couple who settled down there to make a home and a living. In due course the farmer passed away and left his widow to carry on, aided by her young son. Amongst the physical features of the property was a mountain spring which trickled out of a hillside, ice cold and gin clear, filling a hollow in the valley and forming a small lake among the grasses and the flowers. Now the widow was hard put to it to make ends meet, so she bethought herself how she might put this water to profit.

One day the answer came to her. Fish. She would plant fish and breed them. Without more ado she set about it and erected a little hatchery, right there where the water issued fresh from the hillside, so that its first duty should be to run over her trays and give life to her future broods of fish. She erected a little home for herself there, away from the farm-house, for she had fallen in love with the beauty and solitude of the spot and the trickle of the cold water as it passed into her hatchery and out to the little lake beyond. She improved the lake, damming it at its waist so as to raise the water level and give her fish more water and more food. Her scheme prospered, for the soil of the valley was abundant with food, so that her fish grew fat and lusty.

How she turned her fish to profit, whether by way of angling privilege or by the more brutal methods of the fish market I did not ask, though I have had many a talk with her son who is now a well-grown lad of some sixty summers or more, for the widow passed away but a year or two ago. Up to the last she lived there beside her hatchery, which she loved like a child. Her cottage still stands, shuttered and cobwebbed, just as she left it when they carried her away. I think her spirit haunts it still. The son raises potatoes in her garden and sits of an evening by the cottage door, rifle in hand, waiting for the small conies which raid his crop. Once I suggested to him to leave the conies alone and turn his weapon upon the mosquitoes, which seemed fully large enough to shoot.

"Have they worried you?" he asked.

"Indeed they have," I replied. "You have two varieties, a brown and a black. I don't know which is the worse."

"Oh," he remarked, without the vestige of a smile,

"didn't you get any of the yellow ones? Those are the ones that really sting." He said it so seriously that maybe he was speaking the truth; but then again, maybe— I wonder.

She laid the foundation of a great stock of trout, did the old lady; mostly rainbows and brooks. Under the timber bridge below the hatchery, long since disused, I have watched them in the heat of the day, lying in the shade like battle-ships at anchor, awaiting the cool of the evening to go out in search of food. I have seen two dozen or more, not a one under three pounds and many nearer five, lying motionless there. In 1936 I caught a brook of just upon five pounds, on a dry fly, an old Rusty Red tied to a oo hook for me by my old friend Roach of Carter and Co. of London. This year my only fish on the one day I was there was a three-and-a-half-pound rainbow taken on a wet salmon fly; for the day was not propitious and the fish were not showing.

You must pay tribute to the farmer for the privilege, based upon the weight of the fish which you take away. He told me recently that he has received more than one approach about turning the water into a club. I think that would be a good thing, for if too many anglers find it out and take out fish greedily, the quality and romance of the place will go. At the moment, I was given to understand, the government is trying to buy up this and neighbouring farms, in connection, I believe, with a wild bird protection program. Now, I have given you all the clues, as they do in the graphic mystery puzzles. So you may set about finding it for yourself, even as I did, and bring home your own "battle-ship." Don't take more than two, even if you can afford the luxury at so much a pound. One of these giants will suffice to establish your prowess in the eyes of your friends; two will make you a local hero.

I think I have now offered you quite a selection of waters in which to cast your angle. I could tell you of more, of the Red Rock River with its pretty pan fish, of Buffalo Creek, of the North Fork of the Snake, of Warm River, all of them within easy fishing reach of West Yellowstone. Then there is the little river at Ennis which I never identified. I do not think I want to know its name; I like to think of it as "my little river."

I came across it one Sunday. I had driven down the lower Madison, resting, as I fondly hoped, from my rod and line for a day. It was all an accident, as it were. I had lunched in Ennis and on turning out of the town I noticed it, innocently running under a bridge between willow-girt banks, small, unpretentious but pretty as a painting. It was a case of love at first sight. I parked and put up my Hardy "fairy" rod. I selected a brown variant and dropped it on the water at the first bend. Up came a fat little fellow of three quarters of a pound, bright of spots, gay and sporting, like the Breton fish that fell to Fedden in *Golden Days*. Then followed one of those unpremeditated occasions which are the sweetest of all. One after another they came, one after another I gently returned them. They seemed

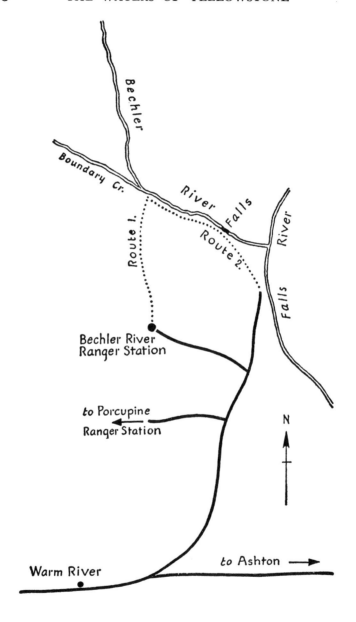

to enjoy the fun as much as I did. I think they felt that I meant them no harm.

Did I tell you on one of your "off" days to drive along the Ashton road to Big Springs? There you may see the birth of a river, bubbling up through the ground amid musk and buttercup, cool with overhanging shade. There you may stand upon the bridge and watch the rainbows sway in the limpid stream in constant expectancy. So when you have eaten at the near-by hostelry, remember to fill your pocket with bread. The fish will be waiting for you, all ready to perform. You shall create your own rise on the "bread fly" and watch them fight for your favours. You may not angle for them, but this is your day "off" so you will be content only to play with them. If ever I saw the Test reborn, it is reborn at Big Springs. That first mile of the North Fork of the Snake is Test in character and quality. So if ever you hear an Englishman boast of his Test, you may reply, "Oh, yes, we have such another stream up in Idaho"; and if he accepts your statement, leave it at that, for beyond the first mile I do not guarantee that your statement will admit of defence!

Bechler River

A moment, please, and an apology. There is a river which I have forgotten and of which I must speak for fear I be accused either of ignorance or of wilful omission.

But for the friendship of Ranger Chapman I might

never have given this river a thought. It was he who
started it. Then Judd Rhoads of the Gallatin Station
chipped in.

"I know a fish up there," he said, "which you could
ride home on, if only you could saddle him."

Well, that was a vivid expression, so I inquired further. It was easy, they said, and I believed them. I now
know that what is easy to a couple of hardy Rangers
may be tough to you and me. I learned that you can't
fish a river until you have got to it, and that you can't
conveniently go to bed until you have got home again.
But my fatal enthusiasm blinded me to these small
points, and away I went.

The Belcher lies in the southwest corner of the
Park. You take the Ashton road out of West Yellowstone and, about two miles after Warm River, or four
miles before you come to Ashton, you turn left on the
brow of a rise along a shell road where stands a picturesque old farm building. This road runs about
twenty miles to a dead end at Falls River, into which
the Bechler flows. A few miles before the end of the
road you will see a road to the left with a sign "To
Bechler River Ranger Station." You have now two
courses open to you. You can run along to the Ranger
Station, park there and make for the river at the point
where Boundary Creek joins it. This is about a four-
mile trek through swamps and rough country. (This is
where my horse will come in the next time!) Alterna-
tively you can go on to the end of the road at Falls
River, park there and cut across to the Bechler *via*

There you may see the birth of a river, bubbling up through the ground amid musk and buttercup, cool with overhanging shade. . . .

. . . There you may stand upon the bridge and watch the rainbows sway in the limpid stream in constant expectancy.

the trail. You then follow the Bechler up some three miles to where Boundary Creek comes in.

Personally I prefer the latter course. You have the advantage of the river beside you all the way, as your guide and comforter; and, if you see a spot that appeals to you, you can stop and fish. However, the big fish are to be had at, and above, where Boundary Creek comes in. There you may well catch a five-pound cut-throat (for it is cutthroat water), and on a dry fly at that. Make no mistake, you will be attacked, *vi et armis,* by a million mosquitoes of the bayonet variety, and you will fall into beaver holes and you will get very hot and tired; but you will see, and I hope catch, big fish. Take a flash-light with you, if you stay in for the evening rise, for you will need it to find your way out. Personally I stayed over night at Ashton, rose at 4 A. M. and went in for the early morning rise. In retrospect I am glad I went, though I am free to admit that when half way home I would willingly have sold you the river with all its contents for two bits.

It is a very beautiful river, so clear and wide that from the shelter of the bank you may watch the fish. You will know them for taking fish by the way they act, heads a little elevated, tails gently swaying, and their whole bodies alert like sprinters waiting for the gun. Yes, in the comfort of my arm-chair I can now well say they were worth it.

CHAPTER SEVEN

IN CONCLUSION, AND WITH SOME SUGGESTIONS

I HAVE stated that this book is not didactic. I have tried to tell you where you may best angle, what fish you may be likely to catch and how you may most easily come to the waterside. I have also tried to tell you something of the beauty of these places, though the fitting words are hard to find. I propose to add some particular experiences of my own and to offer you some pointers as a result of these experiences. They may have some value, either direct or by way of throwing side lights upon some of the problems which face any angler fishing a new water, be he never so competent. I shall close the chapter, and the book, with some suggestions about these waters and the maintenance of their excellence. My criticisms will be tendered humbly, constructively and in the spirit of good sportsmanship. I regard any generation of anglers enjoying the benefits of public waters as trustees for the generations which follow after, and any appeals which I make are made in that belief.

I have in the nature of things conversed with a great many fellow anglers in the course of my riverside wanderings. Generally speaking, the first question which I find put to me, after the preliminary courtesies have

124

been exchanged, is, "What fly are you using?" Now in my opinion there is an erroneous idea prevalent amongst most anglers that the pattern of fly used is the most important feature of the attack. I hold that the way in which the fly is presented and the way in which the water is fished are more contributory to a full creel than the selection of the fly itself. That this selection is important, especially in certain waters, is obvious, but its value should not be over-estimated. Frankly I have found that the fish in the Yellowstone waters are, for the most part, the least particular as to pattern of fly of almost any fish of my experience. I have found that, in wet fly work, size and weight have proved of much greater importance than pattern.

When I first arrived in Yellowstone I carried with me an old selection of flies gathered from many countries. Like every enthusiastic angler, I am possessed of a large number of flies, many of them comparatively useless but all of which have, at some time or other, seemed to me to wear the imprint of success. Some have been purchased in the excitement of the sale room, some after a goodly luncheon at the Club, topped up with a glass of vintage port which always tints my spectacles with rose. Others again have been bought in foreign lands—in Munich, in the Black Forest, in the Jura or the Salzkammergut—in the belief that the local tackle man knows his own fish and their habits best. So in their hundreds they have accumulated over the years, and I cannot be parted from them, except in the course of angling.

Out of these I made selections for trial. In the early days I used a bucktail as my end fly and a small butcher or alexandra as a dropper. For a bucktail I used an "optic" bucktail—that is, one with a bead-dressed head and a large eye painted on it. I have found that this staring eye lends conviction to "an otherwise bald and unconvincing tail"; pardon the pun. I very soon found that the bucktail, which was large, took all the fish, and the smaller dropper was ignored. Was it the pattern of the bucktail or its size that was the cause? I decided to abandon the bucktail and replace it with a fly of about the same size. I searched among the collection and found a fly whose origin I had long since forgotten; it was of the coachman type, peacock herl body, brown hackle and white wings dressed backwards, alderwise. It was tied to a hook which by memory was about a number 6. I put it on and it worked wonders. I got Vint Johnson to dress me a few more like it. The local rage at the time was a squirrel tail which Vint tied admirably and which took innumerable fish. I stuck, however, to my own specialty. That was in the June days when fish were plentiful, and apparently ravenous. It wasn't the pattern, it was the size they were looking to.

Then in July and August came the more difficult days. The fish had been thinned out and they had become wary from much pricking and mishandling. One morning I was fishing the Madison in the meadows when up came a fellow angler and entered into conversation. What fly was I using? I told him.

"You won't catch anything on that," he categorically replied. "There is only one fly to use here for the next few weeks, the Jock Scotch."

With that he opened his fly box and presented me with two flies. Somewhat overcome by his assuredness, by the poetical licence taken with a time-honoured fly title, and still more overcome at the liberties taken with a famous dressing, I muttered appropriate thanks. Shades of Farlow, what a travesty of a Jock Scott! But he proudly claimed fatherhood and went on to state that he charged fifty cents apiece for them! I handed him a dollar and bid him good-day—the old inability to resist buying yet another fly on local recommendation! Of a truth there is an angler born every minute!

Yet I had great value for my dollar. That evening in straightening out my tackle I came upon the two spurious ones. As I looked upon them a sudden light came to me. If this indeed caught fish, what would not a genuine salmon fly do? I rushed to the telegraph office and wired Houston for the early dispatch of two books of salmon flies which I had left behind, never thinking to have use for them. They duly arrived and proved irresistible. I started with size 2 (English scale) and from there I worked on up the scale of sizes. When I left at the end of August I was catching fish freely on size 0. I used a variety of patterns—Durham Rangers, Wilkinsons, Blue Charms, Torridges, Dusty Millers —in fact any and all, as the whim seized me and as my stock provided, using my best judgment according to light, sky and water. My conclusion was that a good range of salmon flies, well and truly tied to pattern, would form the best possible armament for an attack on the Yellowstone trout.

The rashly positive statement of my waterside acquaintance who sold me the Jock Scotts, I mean Scotches, recalled an incident of some years back. He, of course, had business reasons for being so positive, for he wanted to persuade me and make his dollar, but often the superstition of the "ONLY" fly is genuine though unreasoning. I was up in Maine one merry month of May, so decided to try my hand at the famous Bangor pool, of which I had often read. I acquired the services of an excellent gillie named Charlie Bissel, paid my respects and dues to the local salmon club, upped early and proceeded to meet Charlie at the boat shed. It is a big pool and is fished by harling from a boat at every tide.

"What fly shall I put on?" I asked in the cold dawn, for the tide that day was at sunrise.

"We only use one fly here," he replied. "I have put one on; it's all they take."

I examined the fly. I noticed that its prevailing tone was red.

"Well, Charlie," I said, "I am going to give your fish a surprise." Taking out of my book a fly tied for me by Eddie Lyden in Galway, a fly of which the prevailing tone was bright yellow, I tied it on in place of the local wonder, and away we went, Charlie wagging his head gravely and looking almost tearful through the thick pebble of his glasses. Before five minutes were up we were into a beauty, and the pool was agog; for among those intimates I stood out as a stranger. We lost that fish; after a series of splendid acrobatics he came unstuck; but ten minutes later I was into another, a smaller fish which I duly landed.

Charlie, with all the zeal of the convert, was positively apostolic in spreading the news of the yellow fly. Of a sudden Bangor was being combed out for yellow feathers. Any lady who had a hat dressed with one, and an angling husband, did well to put it under lock and key, for an angler's necessity knows no conscience. Probably for the next few weeks the Bangor salmon grew bilious with the sight of yellow flies!

When it comes to a floating imitation of the natural, we enter another field, so pray do not misunderstand me. I have been speaking of wet fly fishing. The abominably selective habits of trout for one type of floating ephemerid are well known and beyond dispute.

To revert to my success with salmon flies, I am convinced that the cause was twofold. Salmon flies are tied to heavy irons, for with a salmon you cannot take a risk of having your hook straightened out. Consequently the weight of the hook takes the fly down to the fish, and that is, to my belief, all-important in these waters. I made one very definite experiment in the Nine Mile Hole. I procured two salmon flies of the same pattern, one tied in America to a light hook for trout fishing and one tied by Farlow of London for Scotch salmon fishing. I first fished the hole down with the light fly and never had a touch. I then went back and came down with the heavy fly. At about the sixth cast I was taken by a big rainbow: he already had the bait hook and gut of some nigger-fisherman in his jaw, so he was not a shy fish. He just had not seen the lighter fly, or, if he had, he would not come up to it. The heavy fly went past his nose and he took it.

Their second merit is their colour range and beauty of action under water, provided of course they are thoroughbreds and not poor substitutes for the genuine article. I believe them, as a whole, to be more irresistible than any other fly, provided size and presentation are right. In a dozen patterns you can carry a range of colour effects suitable for almost every possible condition of water and light.

On the other hand there are objections. They are costly. I should think they would average about a dollar apiece in the sizes required. Then too they are heavy for a light-tipped trout rod, and you don't want to over-rod yourself for three-pound fish; so you must time your cast perfectly. If your fly is at full stretch behind you when you commence the forward stroke, there will be no strain whatever on your rod; so if you use a heavy fly on a light rod, watch your timing. Lastly, if you use the really large size flies, like a o, you will from time to time find yourself losing a fish in the playing and also—if like me you fish without that troublesome article, a landing net, and trust to stranding your fish—you will be apt to lose him at the landing.

For a time this puzzled me, but on reflection the reason became obvious. It lay in the length of the point of the larger size salmon hooks. The point of a salmon hook is designed for the resistance of a fish weighing on an average some 20 pounds. When to the missing of a heart-beat you feel the underwater pull of a salmon, you do not, if you are wise, give a quick strike as you do to a trout. You exert a steady pull against the fish which has turned and is going to the bottom with your fly in his mouth. If you pursue this course, you are justified in expecting that in about as many minutes as he weighs pounds the fish will be lying, all silver and lilac, in the grass at your feet. For the pull and counter pull will have drawn the hook point right in past the barb. When, however, you have but a three-pound trout to pull against, the resistance is not sufficient to set the long point in up to the hilt; so you will in effect be playing your fish on a barbless hook—which is all right with me, since I think it gives good sport and good practice in keeping a tight line on my fish; and, even if he does get off, what of it?

After some years of angling I find myself generally rooting for the fish and, whilst it would be against all sporting traditions to bungle him on purpose, I do not mind creating such odds that the fish has, if anything, the better chance. I am of course not including salmon in this remark. If you resent losing a fish but want to try salmon flies, then I advise you not to go above size 2, English scale. The point of a number 2 will penetrate any trout and the weight of it will take it down to most fish in these waters.

If you are unable or unwilling to take my advice about salmon flies, go into Vint Johnson's shop and ask what is the successful fly of the moment. Any big fish caught are brought in there for display, and it is interesting to note on what they have been caught. I repeat that I don't believe it much matters, so wide is the range of successful flies. What, however, is of great importance is to have confidence in the fly upon which you decide. The man who fishes without the sure belief that he has got "just the thing for them," and is going to catch them, might almost as well stay at home. Confidence in the angler seems, by some telepathic process, to affect the fish. You may laugh at that, but there would seem to be something in it.

I found that it paid to give some action to my fly, not an exaggerated action; a twitch is all that is required, enough to make it dart forward about a foot at a time, not more. I had the impression most of the time that the trout followed me and only took when they feared to lose their prey.

Some fish, on the other hand, had a disconcerting habit of taking the fly with a smash; I can think of no other word to describe it. It was my undoing on many occasions, and I never experienced it in any other water. It is a definite technique of the take. I get the sensation that in these cases the fish would come across and down-stream at high speed, seizing the fly as they passed and snapping it off much as your grocer snaps the string with which he has tied your parcel. I see you smile, but I am encouraged to relate this frequent experience by the fact that I am not alone in it. I have discussed it with Rangers and other competent persons who all recognize it as a local peculiarity and accordingly use strong leaders. For a time it got me very mad, for I had a stock of light leaders which I had to use up. There was a moment when I began to think it would pay to set up a syndicate to placer out the Four Rivers for the recovery of my valuable salmon flies! So use good strong leaders is my advice, honest gut ones if you can afford them, though the Spanish "troubles" have placed the merchandise of Murcia somewhat out of range. I dislike imitation gut intensely; it is as slippery as Uriah Heep and as unreliable as the League of Nations. If you have to use it, make doubly sure of your knots with these fish putting over their smashing rise; it will open up any badly tied knot. A Turle should be the safest, though it is a knot I rarely use.

Please do not misunderstand me, I am not suggesting powerful tackle in order to be able to rough-house your quarry, but only in order to avoid the loss of flies on economical grounds and the leaving of flies in fishes' cheeks on humanitarian grounds; also in this manner you may lose the specimen fish which is above all the one to keep, for it seemed to me to be essentially the big fish which struck in this manner, with weight behind their blow.

I am reminded of one instance which I saw a year or so back of stout tackle and "horsing them in." I was fishing for sea trout one Sunday in the old **Brazos River** at Freeport, Texas, just below the rail-and-road bridge where there is a ten-foot bank behind you and a muddy shore from which you may cast. Just after lunch there drove up behind me on the bluff a car from which stepped a man and a woman. He had the outward appearance of a baseball player with peaked cap and coloured sweater. The lady remained on the bluff with a can of shrimps, which is the recognized bait for this fishing, whilst he came down beside me and commenced to cast. No sooner did he do so than, as at a word of command, by came a shoal of large trout. In a second he was into one, but did he play it? He did not. He just gave one terrific backward jerk with his rod, which must have had a steel centre. The trout "flew through the air with the greatest of ease" into the lap of his waiting partner. Deftly she unhooked it, adjusted a fresh shrimp, shouted "O.K.," and out went the bait again. And so it went, *da capo*. The ball player barely looked round, so well was the act apparently rehearsed. I stood spell-bound watching them, and missed the greater part of one of the best rises of my life.

Then, as suddenly as it had come, the shoal departed, and all was still again. Without a word or a gesture, he climbed the bank, went to the car and, believe it or not, produced two sacks, into which with the aid of his accomplice he tumbled the fish, I should think a good forty of them and not one under two pounds; then into the car they bundled and away. It was all supernatural, their arrival just at the moment of the rise, their apparent expectation of the catch, as witness the sacks, and the calm insouciance with which they packed up and drove away. Were they in league with the powers of darkness? I shall never know. But I shall always marvel at the memory of it, this uncanny instance of "horsing them out."

So once again do not fish with too fine leaders for Hebgen fish, or you will be adding to the dividends of my dredging syndicate; but fish "far," for you must remember that these fish see a great many anglers 'twixt May and October, more than it is good for any fish to see. Many of these anglers seem to be entirely oblivious of the fact that a trout has an exceptionally keen instinct for self-preservation and a system of nerve centres of great delicacy which record the slightest disturbance in its vicinity, and also two eyes which conveniently act independently the one of the other so that it can look in two directions at once, not excluding backwards. So I strongly advise you to move as cautiously as you can, keep as still as you can and cast as far as you can.

If you be free to pick and choose, then I would say come to Yellowstone either at the end of May, when the snow is still on the ground, or at the end of August, when the nights are getting cold and the oncome of winter is already in the air. I have fished in Bavaria in high winter, fished for huchen in the Ammer with Trinks and Dr. Kustermann. I recall we had special rings on our rods, the size of wedding rings, so that we could push our little fingers through and break away the ice which constantly formed and held the lines from running. In our pockets we carried flasks of local firewater which they called *schliebowitz,* though I do not know how they spelled it, to which we resorted at frequent intervals. I remember how we crackled when we left the water for a few minutes, time enough for our waders to freeze upon us. I remember how, when I caught my first huchen, I danced a war dance over its recumbent and glittering form, pretending I was dancing purely from glee when in reality I was dancing to save myself from pneumonia. It was great fun and I never suffered a whit from it, so I do not suppose that the spring fishing in Yellowstone will do you any harm either.

Moreover, in the early spring and in the fall, if what they tell me be true, the mosquitoes are not in evidence. I am frankly sceptical about mosquitoes; I don't believe they have any hundred per cent "off" season. I believe that there are only more mosquitoes or less mosquitoes; I don't believe there are ever NO mosquitoes; but then I am peculiarly sensitive to them.

I devised a method of my own for reducing the trouble. I bought a large coloured handkerchief, or bandanna. This I sewed on to the leather band of my hat so that it fell over my neck and shoulders. I then attached the two sides under my chin with a safety pin, having first anointed it copiously with the best deterrent I could find. Good deterrents are hard to find.

Some of the mosquitoes so take to that they come back, like Oliver, and ask for more. In my experience tar must be one of the components if the resultant concoction is to be really efficacious. In Germany we used to make an emulsion of alcohol and coal tar soap. In a recent number of the *Fishing Gazette* of London I read a prescription cited from *Hunting and Fishing in Canada*. Now I have fished in Canada and know how infernal their pests can be, so maybe this is a good one; I quote it for what it is worth:

3 ounces oil of citronella, 1 ounce oil of spirits of camphor, 1 ounce oil of tar, $\frac{1}{4}$ ounce pennyroyal and 6 ounces castor oil.

Back in my school days there was a book entitled *With Stanley in Darkest Africa*. In that work Stanley is depicted, in Victorian line engraving, wearing a mosquito protector just like mine. It came back to me when I saw myself in the glass. Or should I say that mine is just like his? Anyhow it is efficient, for it leaves only a nun-like section of one's face open to attack; and it overcomes one great problem by protecting the back of the neck. One can defend the face with the forearm and brush off intruders even during the heat of an engagement with *salmo shasta* or any of his cousins, but just try and slap a mosquito on the back of your neck when you are playing a difficult, or any other, fish, and see what happens. You have GOT to let go of something, I mean other than your temper! So take a tip and try the "Stanley" or nun's veil protector. You will thank me.

I did at one time try gloves as well, but I had to give them up. I have, over the years, acquired a knack of retrieving spare line by working it an inch or two at a time through the fingers of my left hand, preparatory to shooting it with the next cast. I found that a glove rendered this movement impossible, and, once I had discarded one glove, the other followed automatically.

A few words with regard to where you may conveniently lodge. My own experience leads to West Yellowstone as being the best centre. From there you can fish, with equal facility, the rivers to the west of the Park and also the outside rivers of which I have spoken, such as the Gallatin and the lower Madison, to mention the two most important, also the South Fork and the lower sections of the Grayling and the Duck. When you decide to fish the Yellowstone, the Lamar or any of the central or southern Park waters, or Slough Creek, then I recommend you to go into the Park and make a stay at Canyon, whilst you are covering this area. The daily ride in and out to these parts from West Yellowstone is slow and tedious, for the road is a dangerous one and calls for careful driving. In Canyon there is an excellent hotel and some clean and comfortable cabins, or you may park your trailer or camp out. There is a cafeteria, a general store, Haynes Book and Picture store, and also a gas station, of which, in my opinion, there are not enough in the Park. So always start your day with a full tank.

West Yellowstone is as friendly a little hamlet as you

will find anywhere. Fishing is its very life and livelihood; it is the language which everyone understands,
the foremost topic of conversation. There are two
hotels and quite a number of cabin camps, also camping grounds. Personally I enjoyed the greatest comfort
and kindness at Wally Bomier's Three Bears Camp. I
can heartily recommend it. The nights are invariably
cool, if not cold, which is a blessing after a hard day's
tramping, for it adds to the perfection of one's rest.
The water is ice cold from the well, the best water I
ever drank, without exception. I never had any use
for ice; two minutes under the tap would ice up anything. You will find that you acquire a personal affection for little West Yellowstone when you have lived
a week or two amongst its friendly folk.

My attempt to tell you something of the angling
wonder-land that is yours is now completed. I know
of nowhere in the world where a man may, for so little
money, enjoy so many miles of first-class trout fishing
in such beautiful surroundings and yet without leaving the beaten track. It is more than probable that
much has escaped me, that many an old angler who
knows the country well could add much to the information I have given you. Yet I do believe that this
work will prove really helpful to intending fishermen.
I know how I would have welcomed it, or something
like it, myself in 1936.

There remains, before I close, one delicate task to
be undertaken—delicate because it may smack of
criticism, though in truth that is not the spirit which

lies behind it. The intention is one of helpful and constructive suggestion, offered only in the interests of good sport and good sportsmanship. These suggestions concern both the angler himself and the authorities, whether Federal or State, to whom are entrusted the care of his interests.

It is a fact beyond question that every year the number of anglers in the United States in general, and in this area in particular, increases by leaps and bounds. Frequent reference to this problem is made by the authorities, by societies, and by the press. That it should be so is a favourable fact, for I doubt if any form of relaxation can better bring relief to the citizen of today, bewildered as he is by the maze of problems in which his life is entangled. I believe that the conservation and preservation of privileges such as those which I have attempted to describe hold an importance for John Citizen greater than many a scheme for his material advancement on which time and money have been spent. I believe that a greater measure of peace within himself will enable him to function better for his own well-being and for that of others. Therefore let us preserve inviolate from any approaching danger, at any reasonable cost, his opportunities of escape and of obtaining that peace within himself.

His tendency in the search of that peace is clearly toward angling. What can be done to meet the consequent and constant increase in the number of anglers? The answer which I almost invariably hear and read is, "Plant more fish." Well and good; it is a partial answer and an answer which is partially sound, but if treated as the absolute and only answer to the problem it at once becomes a mischievous and even a fatal one. It requires qualification. It should read "Plant more fish up to but not beyond the capacity of the water to maintain them." I do not conceive that anyone with even a beginner's knowledge of the care of rivers will deny the soundness of this qualification.

Now clearly there are still in this vast continent waters which can properly hold a larger head of fish than they have at present, especially in the more distant and less frequented areas. Equally there are many in which the limit of reasonable capacity has been reached. What then is the answer in these latter cases? There can be only one answer: "REDUCE THE DAILY LIMIT OF THE CATCH"; and to that you might add a useful corollary: "SEE THAT THE LAW IS UPHELD."

I believe that the Yellowstone district already comes within the category of areas wherein the limit should be reduced, in which statement I do not include the Yellowstone Lake and River, where the limit has already been reduced to five fish per rod per day, as against ten per day in the other waters. Now the fish in all rivers which connect with Hebgen Lake average today about two pounds per fish. I am credibly informed that five years ago the reasonable expectation of average for a day's catch was three pounds. Before that again we have the evidence of the man in the Nine Mile Hole, who caught fifteen fish in a morning, of an average weight of just upon five pounds. I prophesy confidently that in two or three years from now, if the present regulations are upheld, the average will drop to one pound.

Just think a minute what a ten-fish limit means. It means that any angler today may take out of the water TWENTY POUNDS OF TROUT *per diem*. Is that good sense or in any way reasonable? I contend that it is not. I think that the limit should be reduced at once to six fish per rod per day, and that the law should be rigorously enforced.

But, in addition to sound protective legislation and the strict enforcement of that legislation, something else is needed. There is needed the creation of a new spirit among anglers, I do not say all anglers, but among the majority of them; and please do not think I am being critical. I fully realize that the basic trouble is ignorance, ignorance of the difficulty of maintaining a good head of fish in the face of heavy angling. I believe that if the average American angler is led to see the underlying truth of the problem, he will play the game. It is unfair to expect him to alter his code unless you first educate him as to the underlying facts which justify your request. I look for the creation of a new spirit and code, a spirit of admiration not for the man with the overloaded creel but for him who has released all fish beyond his own reasonable requirements. It is all a question of a point of view. I fully realize how humanly chest-expanding it is to empty a full creel before an admiring circle of friends. There is a great kick in it. But THERE IS A GREAT KICK IN THE OTHER POINT OF VIEW IF ONLY YOU CAN ONCE ACQUIRE IT. There is a great kick in taking a fine trout, who has fought you well (remember it is only fun for you but life or death for him), gently removing the hook, holding him firmly behind the pectoral fins, and placing him for a few seconds, head up-stream, in the water, whilst he recovers his breath; then watching life come back, his tail begin to wag, as though in gratitude, and finally seeing him glide away happily into the element from which you took him. There he will be for you, or another, on another day, and you will not be saving just one trout; you will be sponsoring a new form of pride amongst anglers which in time, I hope, will replace the pride in the long string of dead fish. It is only the creation of this new pride which can really preserve the life of these waters as an angling wonder-land for the generations that will come after you. Remember that you are but a life tenant. Remember that to angle is greater than to kill. Remember that the more fish you kill the fewer fish will there be for your angle.

The question of enforcement lies with the authorities who are your trustees, and not with you, except in so far as, if the new pride is born, there will be but little need of enforcement—need only against miscreants, poachers and folk who steal your and my and all citizens' fish for their own personal gain. Yet for the time being it is depressing to see, as I saw, a law-breaker made to pay but a derisory penalty. He was a local man, knew well what he was about, took more fish than the limit allowed, and moreover took them in water which was clearly proclaimed "Closed To Fishing," and yet he was only fined $2.50. Probably when he had sold his illegal catch he was still "up" on balance.

I am credibly informed that in West Yellowstone the Montana authorities maintain only one game warden. That shows great faith in the inhabitants. I only hope it is justified, but if it should not be, this lack of supervision would make an easy opening for anyone who might care to turn a sporting ground into a source of personal financial gain. I am however fully aware that there enters into that problem a question of budget, and I am therefore not criticizing but only wondering.

And now to another point, or rather point of view, for that is all it is. I will stoutly contend with my last breath that a reduction of limit is necessary to the well-being of these waters. I cannot make the same contention about my next suggestion; I can only say that I believe it would be a good thing for the fishing, and I know that this opinion is shared by others who are more entitled than I am to express it. I hold that on most of the rivers in question (I do not say the lakes) fly only should be used. In a recent number of the *Journal of the Fly Fishers' Club of London,* of which society I have long been a member, there is an article entitled "Gentlemen Prefer Flies." I quote its opening paragraph:

Long ago, when the rules of polite society were formulated, it was ordained that Gallant Gentlemen should fish for trout with artificial flies only. This decree, regardless of the fall of dynasties and the overthrow of empires, still stands firm and inviolate.

Now allowing in full for the humour behind the paragraph, I hold that it is a great tenet, and there are many of us, I believe, who subscribe to it. In a practical world, however, there must be an appeal to more than gallantry, for the age of chivalry is dead and gone. There must be an appeal to utility, and it is on the grounds of utility that I think there is good ground for forbidding all lures save artificial flies on the rivers under discussion. The utility resulting from such a ruling would be a reduction in the quantity of fish killed, for in the hands of a fish-killer, as opposed to an angler, the use of the worm, the live bait, the maggot, the spinner or the snatcher lends a decided impetus to slaughter without adding anything to the basic objective of sport. For I assume that we must all admit that sport is the basic objective, and that those who come to Yellowstone to fish do not do so in order to procure their dinner. So if sport is what we are there for, let us use the most sporting method, a method which involves the use of delicate tackle as compared with that to which a worm, live bait or spinner is attached.

I cannot find words which fit with my desire to enlist your sympathy for this philosophy of angling. It is the philosophy at which all seasoned anglers arrive, that the aim and object is to deceive the fish by artifice and with tackle proportioned to the size of the quarry, and that the death of the fish is by no means an essential consequence of the deception. Take by all means what fish you require for your personal use, but ask yourself, when your hand is uplifted to kill, "Am I killing this fish because I need it or do I merely want to show it off to my friends?" If in your heart you cannot deny the latter, then put him gently back into the water and prove yourself a sportsman. If you cannot fool him with a fly, admit like a sportsman that the round is his and go for him all the more skilfully tomorrow. Don't throw worms or masses of revolving metal at him. Sticks of dynamite will kill him too, if that is all you want to achieve; but dynamite has gone out of fashion as part of a trout angler's outfit, so anyway we are making progress. Let us hope that live bait and spinners will come next.

And now for my last suggestion, and this again is one upon the sanity of which I will stake whatever reputation I may have as a student of angling. It concerns Hebgen Lake.

I have stated *ad nauseam* in this book that Hebgen is the heart of the good fishing in the Yellowstone area. But for the capital stock of fish which it protects, the fishing in the rivers which it feeds, seven of them in all, would not be above the ordinary.

In 1936 and 1937 especially heavy withdrawals of water have been necessary, a fact which admits of no criticism but which does call for study and reflection.

What has been the result upon the fish? I am informed that in the fall of 1936 the lake was reduced to a mere channel, that fish lay about stranded in pools and puddles, an easy prey to bird and beast. The same thing must probably have happened in the fall of 1937. Already in the summer of that year the water was exceptionally low. You might fish on foot right down to the Narrows. When the water gets as low as that the fishing in the lake becomes senseless massacre. I have watched fish in the evening swimming around the edge in shoals with their backs out of the water. Any lure cast at the shoal produces a suicidal rush of fish. I saw in a local paper a picture of two anglers holding up a string of twenty perfect fish, all of about two and a half pounds, caught in Hebgen at low water. Some fifty pounds of capital stock trout taken out under conditions which demand no skill whatever; if two anglers do that, you may imagine what the total toll is.

If you, Sir, were left trustee of the estate of a young heir, with full discretionary powers, and he asked you if he and some friends might go gay and "do in" the capital, what would be your reply? You surely would tell him that the income was his to do what he liked with but that not one dollar of the capital should he touch as long as you were responsible for his welfare. Now the fish in Hebgen are capital whilst there. As soon as they run up the rivers, they become dividends. Is it sound, then, to let them be "done in" whilst they are still "capital" and before they come to the dividend stage? I personally believe it to be unsound, particularly seeing to what extremities they have been put over the last two years owing to scarcity of water.

In my humble opinion it would be the act of a wise authority to close Hebgen to fishing entirely during the year 1938 in order to give the capital stock of fish a chance to recuperate from its depredations owing to two successive years of low water. Then after 1938 I think that there should be an automatic ruling under which fishing in Hebgen would immediately stop when and if the water should drop to a given low level, a level of "safety" for the fish, which could be determined with comparative ease.

If Hebgen is thus protected, if the legal limit is reduced and the law is severely enforced, then I believe that this angling district will remain what it is today, even if it does not recover to what it has been in the past. There will be opposition, but it will only be from selfish fishermen who would rather have an unreasonably good time themselves than enjoy fair sport and hand on their privileges unimpaired to their successors. It is from the angling world that the authorities should have support. Any lobbying should be for, and not against, sane measures for protecting this wonderful asset.

Did I say there was not a poisonous snake in this Eden? I was wrong. There is one, as there was in the garden of old. Gentlemen, tread it under your heel. Do not be tempted by the rosy apple of the full creel and the adulation of your friends, and so lose your

Eden; for, once lost, I assure you it is not easily re-gained.

If by writing this book I may have been able to assist a fellow angler in his enjoyment or to enlighten him as to the pleasant places which await him, or if I may have been able by my suggestions to spread the cult of "Spare the fish" to the better preservation of these waters for present and future generations of sportsmen, I shall feel that I have in some small measure paid the debt of gratitude which I owe for happy hours spent beside the waters of Yellowstone, my feet among the flowers and my eyes upon the hills. It has indeed been a beautiful experience. "It was all very exciting."

THE END

AFTERWORD

Who was Howard Back? The answer to that question has the ingredients of a novel. It's not a Victorian melodrama, but a twentieth-century modernist tale of loss and disillusionment. Scott Fitzgerald could have written it, or Hemingway. It could have been filmed in Hollywood. But it's neither fiction nor film, it's fact, and this is where our story begins.

Howard Back learned to fish the fly for trout as a boy, coached by a family friend, on the little River Chess, then a noted chalkstream. The Chess was near the home where he was born in 1882, in a village a few miles northwest of London. He was the third of four brothers, with two younger sisters, in an upper middle-class family.

Family legend has it there was a close link with the great Duke of Wellington, who, on the eve of Waterloo in 1815, asked one of his young lieutenants, a Back, to marry a girl who was carrying the Duke's illegitimate child. A century later young Back lieutenants in the Great War would be called on for greater sacrifices. Howard Back was directly related to Captain Sir George Back, Royal Navy (1796–1878), an explorer of arctic Canada at various times from 1818 to 1837. He was the first person to descend the 600-mile Back River (it is named for him) in the Northwest Territories. His book *Captain Back's Journal, 1833–35, a Narrative of the Arctic Land Expedition* (London 1836) is described in Bruns, *Angling Books of the Americas,* as a "rare and important work."

At age fourteen, Howard Back followed his older brothers, father, and grandfather, to Marlborough College, one of England's great public—that is, private—schools. At Marlborough he continued his trout fishing on the school's stretch of the River Kennet, which, along with the Test and Itchen, is one of the great three English chalkstreams. At Marlborough he was excused from cricket, the college religion, which he thought a dull game; instead, he studied natural history, for which he "had a special bent."

In 1900 Back again followed his father, older brothers, and grandfather to Trinity College, Oxford, being awarded a "commoner exhibition" (a kind of scholarship). At Oxford, he read Classics and helped to found the Savoyard Society, which was devoted to the study of the Gilbert and Sullivan operas. W. S. Gilbert was a friend and neighbor of the Back family. (Back's limpid prose may owe something to his own study of Gilbert and Sullivan. It may also be a testimonial to what John Updike describes as "the curious connection between classical studies and a lean, honed English.") In 1904, Back left Oxford with a disappointing third-class honors degree, possibly owing to prolonged illness prior to taking the degree-qualifying exams.

After leaving Oxford, Back went to work in the office of a railway company at a salary of £100 a year. In 1905, he became engaged to Phyllis Paul, from Scotland, and needed more money than his job provided. So in 1906 he joined the family firm, perhaps reluctantly, of Holmwood, Back and Manson, London insurance brokers, that had been founded by his grandfather. Back prospered in the business and married Phyllis in 1908 in the fashionable London church of St. Paul's, Knightsbridge.

At the onset of the Great War all four brothers entered service, three in the army and one in the Royal Navy. Howard's older brother Horace, a London solicitor, was commissioned a lieutenant in the Gloucester Regiment. He was killed by artillery fire at Mametz Wood in September 1916 on only his third day at the front. Mametz was part of the Battle of the Somme, which began on July 1, 1916; by the time it staggered to a conclusion in the rain and mud in November, British casualties were over 400,000, the French (who had a lesser role in the battle) about 200,000 and the Germans between 400,000 and 500,000. Later, Howard's younger brother, Leonard, was severely wounded in action with the Royal Navy in the North Sea. He never recovered from his wounds and died in 1924.

Howard Back was commissioned a lieutenant in the Royal Engineers, and was often at the front ferrying ammunition and supplies. He referred in *The Waters of Yellowstone with Rod and Fly* to having "witnessed at first hand through two weary years the horrors of modern warfare." The geyser basins of Yellowstone reminded him of the second battle of the Somme as it appeared in 1918. Another transport trooper described the hell of the wet and boggy valley of the Somme battlefield in 1917: the rural roads were now made up of greasy planks "to leave which is to fall into a swamp up to the armpits . . . to remain on it is to pass through accurate and ruthless shell-fire."

The late Ted Hughes, the fine English poet and poet laureate, as well as a fly fisherman, said in a 1965 essay that the First World War is "our number one national ghost." He wrote of the survivors: "They gave their brain-scarred accounts . . . And somewhere in the nervous system of each survivor the underworld of perpetual Somme rages on unabated."

Like his eldest brother Ivor, a battlefield surgeon, Howard escaped the war unscathed physically, but probably not psychologically. In his book, he alluded to the sense of futility and postwar disillusionment (along with millions of others on both sides, the so-called Lost Generation): after "all those four years of tragic imbecility," he "watched the birth of a new world" but it was "a world of greed and cruelty as never before."

At war's end Howard Back came home to further disillusionment; after two years of urging his ammunition vans through the constant mud and shellfire to the trenches, he discovered that Phyllis had been living a high life in café society with intimations of infidelity. The war destroyed more than its combatants. Coping with a great wound of disillusionment is like grieving—everyone does it their own way. Ivor withdrew to Scotland and lived there quietly the rest of his life. Howard and Phyllis parted with a bitter divorce in 1920.

One way to escape the world, paradoxically, is to plunge into it. Coping with his own brain-scarred account, Howard immersed himself in the family business. (Art imitates life. Allan Gurganus, in his short story "He's at the Office," tells how the father in the story enlisted with "three other guys" from his hometown, and was the only one to return "alive with all his limbs." "You can't blame mustard gas," his wife says, "not this time. It's more what Dick saw. He came home and he was all business.") Back was so successful at business that he was able to devote much time to acquiring a large collection of rare and valuable pieces of Chinese art. (Who else could compare the color and sheen of rainbow trout to Kang Shi and Wan Li porcelain vases?)

Back's father, Formby Back, had important business interests in Cairo, Egypt, in newspapers, insurance, and the Shepherd's Hotel, one of the most famous of the British overseas hotels. (Its only peer was the Raffles Hotel in Singapore.) Formby Back died in 1913 and Howard pursued the family's business interests there—noting in his book that he had spent no small part of his life in Egypt. British social circles in Cairo brought him into contact with Howard Carter, the prominent Egyptologist. Back accompanied Carter on the 1922 expedition into the Valley of the Kings that found King Tutankhamen's Tomb virtually intact. (In *The Waters of Yellowstone* he compared the beaded rig used to troll for North American lake trout with a necklace out of the tomb; he had been there, he knew.)

"I am, alas, still at the bottom of the second class as an angler," Howard Back lamented at the beginning of his book, but he claimed "to be at the top of the first class as an angling enthusiast." However he may have modestly downgraded his skill, there is no doubting his passion for the sport. His business success in the family's insurance firm and also as an underwriting member of Lloyd's of London, the famous shipping and specialty insurers, gave Back the resources to fish often and anywhere.

As Back records in his book, he had "varied and extensive fishing experience." He fished in England, Scotland, and Ireland, on the European continent, and later in North America. He fished the Bourne, "a little Hampshire chalk stream," he noted, "tributary of the famous Test, many a happy time." The Bourne is the subject of Harry Plunkett-Greene's famous book, *Where the Bright Waters Meet:* "one of the most beautiful books of angling ever penned," Back observed; the book still deserves such praise. He tells us he read all angling books "or all of which I become aware." Back fished often on the Test with his friend Leander McCormick (author of *Fishing Round the World*, 1937). Jack Hemingway also knew McCormick and said in his memoir that McCormick helped him with his casting.

Salmon claimed much of Back's attention and he went regularly to Scotland to fish for them. He cannot resist telling us (who could?) about the forty-six-pounder he caught in the River Don. He sometimes fished with the legendary Charles Ritz on the continent and in England on the Test. He fished in Bavaria and Austria for grayling, in Yugoslavia, and in Bavaria for huchen with the prominent German angler, Dr. Kustermann, who figured much in Ritz's book, *A Fly Fisher's Life*.

The techniques Back used were typical of those used by serious fly fishermen of his time: dry fly and wet fly for trout according to the stream and conditions, and wet fly for salmon. He may have been one of the first nymph fishermen in the United States. He detested bait and especially spinners, describing the latter as "ironmongery."

In England, Back was a member of the famous Flyfishers' Club of London, whose members included Halford, Skues, and many other prominent anglers, and he maintained his membership after emigration. He was later to join its sister club, the Anglers' Club of New York.

In his book, Back said he "learned that, if blood be thicker than water, money is thicker than blood." His wealth from his success in the family firm and with Lloyd's, caused family relations to become acrimonious. ("Other family members behaved badly," his daughter says.) In 1928, he married Josephine (the beloved Jo of the book's dedication) who was from a wealthy German family with homes in both Germany and London. Apparently because of the family money frictions and his general disillusionment after the war, Back decided to emigrate to New York in 1930 and continue his insurance business there. The marriage to Jo may have contributed to the decision since Germans were not accepted in postwar London, but Howard's daughter says that Jo was "nice enough to overcome that." Of his two children, his son Denys had been living with his mother in Scotland; his daughter, Betty, who was being raised by one of Howard's sisters, moved regularly between England and the United States after her father emigrated.

Back invested heavily in a speculative Texas oil scheme that proved financially disastrous. (He was taken by some wildcatter sharpies.) At some point he moved to Houston, presumably because of his oil investment. When he moved is uncertain; in 1935 he still listed a New York address in the Anglers' Club directory. But he maintained homes in New York City and Houston for a time. Jo died, suddenly, in 1935 in Houston, leaving Back devastated. In the book, he said that he had "lost the one wonderful person (who) made full compensation for all life's bitter deceptions."

In his grief, Back escaped to the Yellowstone high country in the summers of 1936 and 1937 for weeks at a time, accompanied only by his dog, and following the 1937 trip, he wrote his book. It went largely unnoticed:

154

There was one printing probably only of about 1,500 copies. The estimate of such a small press run is supported by the used book dealer prices. The book appears infrequently in such lists, but the latest price I have seen for a copy, without a dust jacket, was $250. Judith Bowman, a leading dealer in used, rare, and out-of-print sporting books, says she has seen only eleven copies in twenty years in the business.

Ranger (Scotty) Chapman, who was Back's mentor in the Park, went over the whole draft manuscript with Back. Chapman, who still lives near the Park, figured in the book and in Ray Bergman's *Trout* and, especially, in Datus Proper's *What the Trout Said.*

The widest notice given to the book that I am aware of was by Charles Brooks, who included it in his list of forty "books of special merit" in his chapter on "Reading for the Serious Angler" in his excellent 1974 book, *The Trout and the Stream.* Jack Hemingway bought the book in 1939 at Yellowstone Park and mentioned in his 1986 memoir, *Misadventures of a Fly Fisherman,* how it had guided his fishing. Later, in an introduction to a pictorial book, *Flywater,* by McClintock and Crockett (1994) he refers to it as "a fabulous little book."

Although what Howard Back had to say about Yellowstone waters is still of value, there are more up-to-date and more comprehensive guidebooks to Yellowstone country fishing available now. So why should we read it today? Charles Brooks described it as a "charming small book . . . that is totally delightful." And that is the merit of Howard Back's little 149-page book. It has something mesmerizing about it, a fey quality that puts you under a spell. There is a "romance that lies deep in all of us disguise it how we will," Howard Back said. He reveals his own romance when he writes that he has "been unable to live in the beauty of Yellowstone without feeling the touch of fairies' wings as they flitted from flower to flower." He is not tongue in cheek or just being fanciful. When we read his book, we, too, can feel "the touch of fairies' wings." Howard Back transformed the prosaic guide book into a charming pastoral.

Back returned to New York about 1938 and entered the fine arts and antiques business; a subject he knew well and was good at. (Over the years he had extended his interest to painting and became a connoisseur of European old masters.) He co-founded and ran the Kende Gallery, an art auction house in New York City, and he became vice-president of the Art and Antique Dealers League of America. In the early 1940s he married again: Maureen ("Mo") Calloway, who had been his secretary. We know nothing of his fishing after his return to New York, and he died there on 14 November 1946, age only sixty-four.

At the end of his book, Back said that he hoped it would "in some small measure [pay] the debt of gratitude" he felt for the happy time he spent "beside the waters of Yellowstone, my feet among the flowers and my eyes upon the hills." The ledger is closed on that one. His book will be read as long as there are Americans who pick up a fly rod.

In Evelyn Waugh's *Brideshead Revisited* one of the characters rebukes the narrator, an artist, for painting charmingly. Charm, he says, "kills love and it kills art." But Howard Back wrote charmingly without being cloying, and he knew art and he knew love. His ashes were sent to England where his daughter scattered them on the River Chess where our story began.

Acknowledgment

I am grateful for the extensive and enthusiastic assistance provided by Howard Back's grandsons, Michael and Peter Davis of London, keen fly fishers both, as we jointly explored their grandfather's story. Without their help and that of their mother, Howard Back's daughter, Betty Back Davis (an avid fly fisher herself, who taught her two sons to fish), there would be no story to tell.

ROBERT H. BERLS